MW01253088

Criminal Justice
Recent Scholarship

Edited by
Marilyn McShane and Frank P. Williams III

A Series from LFB Scholarly

Understanding Homicide Trends
The Social Context of a Homicide Epidemic

Benjamin Pearson-Nelson

LFB Scholarly Publishing LLC
New York 2008

Library of Congress Cataloging-in-Publication Data

Pearson-Nelson, Benjamin, 1978-
  Understanding homicide trends : the social context of a homicide epidemic / Benjamin Pearson-Nelson.
      p. cm. -- (Criminal justice : recent scholarship)
  Includes bibliographical references and index.
  ISBN 978-1-59332-263-2 (alk. paper)
  1. Homicide--United States. 2. Drug abuse and crime--United States.
3. Population density--United States. 4. Cocaine abuse--United States.
5. Crime forecasting--United States. I. Title.
  HV6529.P43 2008
  364.1520973--dc22

2007050636

ISBN 978-1-59332-263-2

Printed on acid-free 250-year-life paper.

Manufactured in the United States of America.

TABLE OF CONTENTS

ACKNOWLEDGEMENTS

Writing a book is an activity that requires a great deal more time, energy, and sacrifice than one might expect. The activity also requires a cast of characters that goes well beyond whoever gets ultimate credit for authorship. This book is no exception.

Dr. Steven F. Messner deserves a lion's share of the credit for patiently encouraging the production of the text and for thoughtful criticism and suggestions that have improved this book well beyond the original drafts. A host of scholars also joined the chorus: Dr. Paul E. Nelson, Julie A. Seitz, and James Stevens, all read earlier drafts and offered their critiques and ideas for the development of the book. I truly appreciate the work of those who stood behind me and this book.

PREFACE

Homicide is a crime that strikes fear into the hearts of Americans. We see homicides on television, read about them in newspapers, and even the media we consume purely for entertainment is fraught with murder. However, despite the seeming ubiquitous nature of homicide, much about this crime remains mysterious. Criminologists can tell you what groups of people are the more likely to be homicide offenders and what areas of a city are the most likely to have higher rates of homicide. Yet, when homicides increase in our cities, we scramble for explanations.

Police and politicians claim to be able to prevent homicide. They will gladly take credit whenever homicide rates decline. On the other hand, they are conspicuously powerless when homicide rates increase. The truth is: criminologists lack a thorough understanding of how trends in homicide operate. Our reliance on cross-sectional data is partly to blame. Our inattention to changes in trends over time is also a problem. This book is a step toward uncovering what causes homicide rates to change over time. The focus of the book is time in recent memory when homicide rates increased drastically, a period commonly called a homicide epidemic. Luckily, homicide rates fell after peaking at a historically high level. The benefit of lower homicide rates is that now the trends can be studied in a sober and systematic way, without the distraction of impulsive clamor. The pages that follow tell the story of what caused a frightening period of increasing homicides. The overarching goal of this book is to better understand changes in homicide rates, before the next epidemic strikes.

CHAPTER 1

An Epidemic of Violence: U.S. Homicide Trends

Imagine a large city just at introduction of a deadly communicable disease. The outbreak begins with just a few early cases. These early cases are then followed by a trickle that eventually leads to a torrent of dead bodies. But this disease does not affect everyone equally, the youth of the city are the main victims. Soon throughout the city young people disappear from the landscape as the morgue fills.

Now imagine that instead of a disease, the early adopters instead introduce handguns into the populous. And the handguns spread in much the same way, first a trickle and then a torrent. Soon, young people throughout the city are armed. Now, disputes between boys that once ended with bloody noses end with lethal violence. Young men die at unprecedented rates.

The diffusion of guns and violence through a city seems like the plot of a Hollywood movie, but this book will tell the story of just such a time. In fact, the diffusion of violence that took place in the United States plagued cities across the country. The story is an important one because the violence that marked this period is not well understood. As the bodies of young people stacked up, public officials scrambled to stem the tide. Luckily, the flood of homicides peaked and then declined to levels that seemed more manageable. However, the probability of another homicide epidemic is high. The question is, will we have learned anything in this period of relative calm to help us during the next outbreak?

The homicide rate in the United States has undergone considerable fluctuation over the last few decades. Since the latter half of the 1990s, the homicide rate has declined and remains relatively low. However, the country experienced a period in the late 1980s and early 1990s in which the national homicide rate increased rapidly and then peaked at a high level. Scholars of both crime and public health have identified this period as a homicide epidemic. While lower homicide rates since the mid-1990s may support some level of optimism about the general homicide rate trend, a clear understanding of the homicide epidemic of the late 1980s and early 1990s remains elusive.

This book will discuss tests of the effects of key variables, including measures of city population size, population density, population composition, and resource deprivation as well the per capita number of police and on the presence, magnitude, and duration of the homicide epidemic within major American cities. Traditional criminological theories-such as anomie theory and social disorganization theory-indicate that variables such as resource deprivation are positively related to crime rates. However, rapid changes in crime rates are generally not within the scope of conventional criminological theories. Contemporary theorizing attempts to overcome this weakness in explaining the homicide epidemic period (e.g., Blumstein 1995, Blumstein and Rosenfeld 1998, Cook and Laub 1998, Zimring and Hawkins 1997). The research presented here tests explanations drawn from current theories and helps to determine the efficacy of major social structural variables and public policy variables for explaining variation in the presence, duration, and magnitude of the homicide epidemic for major cities. Additionally, this research tests the relationship between the proximity of cities to major cocaine distribution hubs and variation in the three parameters of the epidemic. The United States Census, the Uniform Crime Reporting Program, National Drug Intelligence Center reports, and other supplemental administrative sources provided data for this research.

What has research revealed about the homicide epidemic? Research has uncovered important characteristics of the epidemic. One of the most fruitful approaches to disentangling the conditions that led to the homicide epidemic has been to disaggregate homicide rates by age, race, and gender. An alternative method of disaggregation is to consider the importance of geography. Researchers continue to highlight major cities as the key focal points for the homicide epidemic.

Scholars have conducted some research on intercity variation in homicide rates. A common approach to understanding the importance of city size is to test categories of cities aggregated by population size. However, little research explores the causes of inter-city variation in important attributes of the homicide epidemic.

Actually, the presence, magnitude, and duration of the homicide increases vary greatly during this period. For instance, city-level homicide rates reveal that many major American cities actually did not experience an epidemic during this time period. On the other hand, some cities experienced increases that lasted over a decade. The overarching question guiding this book is: Can scholarship explain city-level variation in the homicide epidemic parameters?

The United States has the dubious distinction of having the highest homicide rate among industrialized nations and one of the highest homicide rates in the world. This distinction has not gone unnoticed by the American media or its citizens. Indeed, Zimring and Hawkins (1997) argue that the high levels of lethal violence in the United States are "a distinct social problem that is the real source of fear and anger in American life" (3). The high levels of violence continue to draw the interest of criminologists and public health researchers.

The notion that the United States suffers from unusually high rates of violence is especially alarming during periods when rates unexpectedly increase at a rapid pace[1]. Such a period could be called an epidemic. The conceptual definition of an epidemic will be discussed in greater detail in the next chapter, but the generally accepted definition among epidemiologists is that an epidemic is a period of time in which the rate of a phenomenon of interest is higher than would be expected based on the general rate trend.

What value can be derived from using the concept *epidemic* to explain homicide rate variation? After all, the term *epidemic* is most commonly used in the public health literature to refer to diseases, a group of phenomena that seems unrelated to homicide. In fact, criminology can greatly benefit from utilizing the epidemiological approach to better understand the spatial diffusion of rate increases for crimes such as homicide. Epidemiology has developed a conceptual language and distinct approach that sheds light on the way that homicide rates operate within national boundaries.

What value does an epidemiological approach have for criminologists? The theoretical frameworks developed in criminology do not explain periods of rapid change in crime rates in the absence of rapid structural or cultural change. To be sure, what research has revealed about the causes of homicide rates provides a necessary foundation for the study of homicide epidemics. Theories about the causes of increased rates of violence have led to a number of valuable discoveries. However, elements drawn from theoretical frameworks aimed at elucidating the causes of rapidly inclining rates over time and across space can help explain the ways in which national crime trends operate. Furthermore, criminologists have already begun synthesizing the public health approach to understanding violence to explain changes in crime rate trends (see e.g., Moore 1995 and Weiss 1996).

In fact, in an essay on youth violence during the late 1980s and early 1990s, Cook and Laub (1998) note, "...the volatility of youth-violence rates makes predictions of any sort highly uncertain. The run-up has been more akin to an outbreak of some contagious disease than to a conventional secular trend" (28). Furthermore, the term *epidemic* has been used with some regularity to describe both homicide and youth violence in general (e.g., Cook and Laub 1998, Moore and Tonry 1998).

A common epidemiological definition of *epidemic* is an "unusually high incidence of a disease where 'unusually high' is fixed in time, in space, and in the persons afflicted as compared with previous experience" (Hagget 2000, 2). The phrase "unusually high" does not necessitate an *explosive* increase, which might be expected for some contagious outbreaks. Other diffusion patterns also meet the criteria for this definition. For example, a *steady* increase in rates beyond what is expected can also be classified as an epidemic. Furthermore, even a contagious pattern of diffusion also does not necessitate an explosive increase. Rather a steady spread of increases in rates radiating from central areas can be classified as an epidemic with a contagious pattern diffusion, as long as the increase in rates is unusually high. The attributes of "processes of diffusion" will be discussed in detail in the next chapter.

The most recent national homicide epidemic spawned numerous research projects seeking causes on the increase in rates (e.g., Blumstein 1995, Blumstein and Rosenfeld 1998, Cook and Laub 1998, Cork 1999, Rosenfeld 2002, Tonry and Moore 1998) and on the causes of the decline that followed in the early to mid 1990s (e.g., Blumstein and Wallman 2000, Cook and Laub 2002, Conklin 2003).

Explanations for the increase in homicide rates have included an increase in young male "super predators" (Bennett et al. 1996), the growth of a relatively large cohort of young males (O'Brien et al. 1999, O'Brien and Stockard 2003), the introduction and diffusion of crack cocaine (e.g., Baumer 1994, Ousey and Lee 2002), and an increase in the demand for firearms following the introduction of crack cocaine (e.g., Blumstein 1995, Cork 1999, Grogger and Willis 2000). Not all of these explanations are fully developed theories. The next chapters of this book will discuss the theoretical and empirical work in greater detail, and I will outline Blumstein's theory in chapter 2, a theory which calls specific attention to homicide rate changes and the role of crack cocaine in urban areas.

Some of the explanations proposed for the incline in homicide rates can also be applied in a symmetrical fashion to the decline. Examples include the introduction of a large cohort of young males, followed years later by their "aging out" of crime, and the introduction of crack cocaine, followed by a later decline in users. However, the decline in homicide rates has also been attributed to causes that are seemingly unrelated to the incline such as aggressive policing strategies (Kelling and Bratton 1998), increasing incarceration rates, and even a tenuous connection to increases in abortions in the early 1970s (Donohue and Levitt 2001).

Experts have not reached a consensus on the causes of the homicide epidemic, but the dominant explanation is Blumstein's (1995) thesis that homicide rates increased as the use and sale of crack cocaine spread across the United States. As young drug dealers armed themselves and disputes became increasingly violent (and lethal), even youth not directly involved with the drug trade were more likely to arm themselves for protection. This urban "arms race" led to concurrent increases in the homicide rate.

This theory has received some support. Recent research indicates that the increase in homicides that began in the mid-1980s can be attributed to an increase in youth homicide caused by firearms (Cook and Laub 1998, Cork 1999). We know that disaggregating the national homicide rate by age groups, sex, and race reveals that young male minority offenders and victims primarily drove the increase in rates[2]. As Cook and Laub note:

> The epidemic of violence that began in the mid-1980s was of unprecedented intensity, but narrowly channeled, like a flood in a canyon; most of those caught up in this epidemic, either as victims or perpetrators, were young black or Hispanic males. That flood peaked in 1993-94 and receded since. The huge swing in rates—a tripling of the homicide-commission rate by adolescents over just eight years—is a challenge to existing theories of the determinants of violence (2002, 2).

Indeed, many of the theories that have been purposed for the homicide epidemic, including Blumstein's, are *ad hoc*. However, one notable extension to the theory of the drugs-violence nexus does draw on research from mainstream criminological theory. One hypothesis drawn from Zimring and Hawkins' (1997) theory of contingent causation is that homicide rate increases are caused not just by the emergence of a drug market, such as the crack cocaine market. Instead, this hypothesis indicates that homicide rates will increase with the introduction of illegal drug markets in areas that have preexisting social factors that are positively related to violent behavior. This hypothesis is an important addition to the debate since some experts doubt that inter-city variation in homicide trends precisely followed the inter-city diffusion of crack (Cook and Laub 1998). One of the challenges confronted in this book is to determine how variables associated with increased levels of violence may have influenced the presence, magnitude, and duration of the homicide epidemic.

Blumstein's (1995) theory on the cause of the homicide epidemic remains prevalent, in part, because it explains the symmetry of the rapid increase and the decline. This theory has also received empirical support. Some key hypotheses drawn from Blumstein's work concerning the diffusion of homicide rates have already been addressed. Cork's (1999) work is one of the best examples of a test of Blumstein's theory. Cork used an innovation diffusion model with city-level data to connect crack markets to the increase in homicides by handguns. Cork found that homicide rates increased in a pattern similar to the increases in crack consumption subsequent to the introduction of crack. Messner et al. (2003) looked at the timing of the homicide epidemic and found support for the general hypotheses that large cities and coastal cities were among the first to experience the homicide epidemic. Messner et al. also point out that while almost half of the cities in their sample of 70 major U.S. cities showed evidence of a homicide epidemic between 1980 and 2000, the timing of homicide rate patterns of individual cities varied widely, and many did not experience an epidemic during this time period. I will review the extant research on the homicide epidemic period in chapter 3.

However, a number of interesting questions about the homicide epidemic have not yet been explored. Questions remain about important attributes of the diffusion pattern followed by the homicide rate increases. Why did some major American cities experience the epidemic, while others did not? Did larger cities have homicide rate increases of greater magnitude than smaller cities? Did the largest cities experience the longest epidemic cycles?

Zimring and Hawkins' hypothesis that preexisting social conditions influence the levels of violence associated with emerging drug markets raises additional questions. Did social conditions related to violence influence the presence of the homicide epidemic? Did these same conditions influence the magnitude and duration of the epidemic? What about the suggestion from advocates of policing that increasing the number of police officers can ameliorate lethal violence? I will systematically answer these questions in this book.

This book takes a somewhat unusual tack on city-level variation homicide rate variation during the recent epidemic period. First, I will discuss the ways in which epidemiological concepts have influenced the study of the homicide epidemic. Then I will discuss the theoretical and empirical work related to the homicide epidemic. I will test hypotheses drawn from Blumstein's (1995) theory on the relationship between crack cocaine and the homicide epidemic and from Zimring and Hawkins' (1997) theory of contingent causation. Synthesizing these theories provides a useful framework for explaining important attributes of the homicide epidemic. I will also look at the per capita number of police, which may have served to counteract the spread of the epidemic.

I will test a number of key exogenous variables to determine how they may have affected three parameters: the likelihood that a city experienced the epidemic and, for cities that experienced the epidemic, the variation in magnitude, and duration of the epidemic. The exogenous variables will include measures of city size, population density and composition, resource deprivation, and the number of police.

The first step in this process is to determine which major American cities actually experienced the homicide epidemic. The process of determining which cities experienced the epidemic is not as straightforward as it may seem. Making judgments by simply looking at plots of homicide rates disaggregated to the city level is somewhat misleading since the rates are often highly volatile. To determine exactly what point a period of increase begins and ends is difficult.

One solution to this problem is to adopt a statistically sound approach to removing the "noise" that masks the "true" rate of homicide. For example, spline regression can be applied to the official rate trends to smooth the patterns and reveal key points of departure from the general trend. Adopting this approach reveals which cities experienced the epidemic, and for cities that experience the epidemic, how great the increase was and how long the epidemic lasted. Spline regression is the approach used by Messner et al. (2003) to determine which cities were in the vanguard of increasing homicide rates during the epidemic period. Spline regression techniques will be explained in greater detail in chapter 4.

Once I determine the homicide rate patterns for each city, I will test which cities experienced epidemics of the greatest magnitude and for the longest duration. While Messner et al. (2003) have identified important aspects of the timing of the epidemic for major cities, they did not test for variations in magnitude or duration. Finally, I will test the effects of exogenous variables that may have created an urban environment that is at greater risk for experiencing a homicide epidemic. I will use logistic regression to test the effects of these variables on the likelihood of cities experiencing the epidemic. For cities with the epidemic I will use regression tests, including Tobit regressions, to detect variations in magnitude and duration of the epidemic cycle caused by the key exogenous variables.

In addition to filling a gap in the literature on homicide epidemics by testing the effects of important social and public policy variables on the parameters of diffusion patterns of the epidemic this research will help to inform the public debate on solutions to the problem of high levels of lethal violence. Uncovering the effect of crucial variables on the parameters of the diffusion pattern at the city level will provide important insights into what sorts of public reactions are most likely to retard the diffusion of homicide rates, as well as highlighting which variables increase the vulnerability of cities to the spread of violence. Finding out which variables have the greatest effect on the likelihood of a city experiencing a homicide epidemic and how these variables affect the magnitude and duration of the epidemic will allow us to better evaluate current policies aimed at reducing urban violence.

While a number of studies have already analyzed the homicide epidemic of the late 1980s and early 1990s, I extend the findings beyond the current literature in several ways. First, I compare the characteristics of cities that did not experience the epidemic with those that did. This comparison is a key extension of the current city-level research on the homicide epidemic. The extant research on the national homicide epidemic is primarily concerned with which social groups were at the greatest risk, what types of homicide increased, the relationship between the victim and the offender, and the type of weapon involved. City-level research on the epidemic identifies which cities began and ended the epidemic first, the relationship between the increase in crack cocaine and the increase in homicide rates, and the contingent effects of resource deprivation on the relationship between cocaine and homicide.

City-level research on the epidemic period to date has focused almost exclusively on cities that experienced the epidemic, while ignoring cities that did not experience the epidemic. This fact is not particularly surprising, since criminology is primarily concerned with explaining the presence, not the absence, of criminal activity. However, uncovering the fundamental differences between cities that did and did not experience the epidemic can help us to understand what variables are related to the presence of the epidemic, which may help predict which cities are most vulnerable to the diffusion of future epidemics.

I also go beyond the extant research on the epidemic period by analyzing the effects of key city-level variables on the magnitude and duration of the epidemic. No research to date explores city-level variation in these two parameters. Greater understanding of the variables that affect these parameters will help us to ascertain why some cities experienced a homicide epidemic of great proportions, while other cities experienced relatively mild epidemic periods. Another goal of this book is to determine whether or not the same variables affect the magnitude and duration of the epidemic in the same way.

Finally, I look at the role of the number of police on the magnitude and duration of the epidemic. The empirical data on the relationship between policing and violent crime has not produced consistent findings (for a review of this literature see Eck and Maguire 2000). This book relies on the number of police per capita to measure the effects of policing. The number of police officers per capita is a measure that has received empirical support as a significant variable in explaining crime rate declines (Levitt 2004). While this approach does not entirely eliminate endogeniety issues (i.e., does increasing the number of police officers affect homicide rates or do homicide rates affect the number of police officers or are the effects reciprocal?), the tests included in this book will provide an analysis of the relationship between the number of police and the characteristics of the epidemic.

The general approach of this book represents a significant extension of previous research on the homicide epidemic because it relies on a fusion of concepts and ideas from the field of epidemiology with subject matter that has been most thoroughly explored by criminology. Combining the approaches of these two disparate fields should shed new light on how homicide rate changes operate, which should help to determine the causes of homicide rate increases, as well as the effectiveness of countering rate increases with policing.

CHAPTER 2

The Homicide Epidemic: Crafting a Theoretical Framework

Criminologists have exhibited considerable interest in the burgeoning homicide rates of the late 1980s and early 1990s. Research into the nature and causes of the rapid increase has revealed valuable information about which demographic groups experienced the highest levels of lethal violence and which categories of homicide increased to the greatest degree. Blumstein's (1995) thesis, which indicates a relationship between the rise and fall of the crack cocaine market and the rise and fall in homicide rates, remains the most popular explanation for the rate shifts and has received support from a number of studies.

An emerging avenue of research on the homicide epidemic is uncovering the nature of the diffusion patterns followed by the epidemic. When the national homicide rate is disaggregated by individual cities, noteworthy differences emerge in the homicide trends both in timing and level of change. Blumstein has attributed the trend differences to variations in the spread and concentration of the crack cocaine market, which is linked to city-level characteristics including geographic location and size. Statistical tests on city-level characteristics and the homicide rate trends indicate that Blumstein's assertions are plausible.

Researchers have already explored the diffusion of the homicide epidemic by examining geographic characteristics, the timing of the initial incline and decline, and the increased vulnerability of the largest American cities (e.g.,Blumstein 1995, Blumstein and Rosenfeld 1998,

Cook and Laub 1998, Cork 1999, Messner et al. 2005, Rosenfeld 2002). However, key questions about the homicide epidemic remain unexamined.

This book explores three important questions about the homicide epidemic that remain unanswered. Three fundamental questions are examined in this book:

1. Why did some major American cities experience the homicide epidemic, while others did not?

2. What caused the variation in the magnitude of rate changes for different cities during the homicide epidemic period?

3. What caused the variation in the duration of the epidemic cycle for different cities?

These questions highlight three important parameters of the homicide epidemic period that have not yet been thoroughly considered at the city level: the presence, the magnitude, and the duration.

To date no one has developed a comprehensive theoretical framework that explains the pattern of change that occurs in periods of rapid crime diffusion. Although contemporary crime theories do not account for rapid crime trend change, the field of epidemiology is uniquely suited to explaining such changes. Although the criminological literature borrows terms like *contagion*, *epidemic*, and *outbreak*, scholars have only rarely applied these terms to social phenomena (for a notable exception on the term *epidemic* see Moore and Tonry 1998).

The concept *epidemic* illustrates this point. At times scholars use this concept to convey the intensity of a social problem that may seem especially poignant at the moment, such as an "epidemic" of school shootings. However, this usage, while common, often refers to phenomena that lack the technical characteristics associated with the epidemiological and statistical definition of an epidemic. The epidemiological concept of epidemic implies, among other things, distinct patterns of disease diffusion.

The epidemiological approach also calls attention to the importance of the geographic and social structural environment in which an epidemic occurs. The purpose of this book is to carefully examine key social variables in cities in which the homicide epidemic occurred and also in cities in which the epidemic did not occur. What is the relationship between crime rate changes and social context? This study uncovers which social variables affect diffusion patterns of homicide to answer that question. Determining which social variables affect patterns of the diffusion of crimes such as homicide will help to clarify the relationship between crime rate changes and social context.

The field of epidemiology has a long history of focusing on variables that help or hinder the diffusion of disease. This approach has proven valuable in understanding the nature of diseases and in combating the spread of disease. The importance of social context has also received attention within the field of criminology, ranging from classical social disorganization theory to the more recent contributions of routine activities theory. Some of the concepts and approaches used in the field of epidemiology are also useful for understanding criminal activity. Adapting such concepts and approaches seems especially valuable in research on crimes that are also considered public health issues such as homicide and suicide. The fusion of public health perspectives with criminal justice approaches is an area that has seen increased growth in recent years, and this synthesis has the potential to increase the ability of criminological research to inform programs aimed at preventing violence (see e.g., Moore 1995).

Applying Epidemiological Concepts

What are the key concepts in epidemiology that criminologists can apply to the causes, presence, and diffusion of the homicide epidemic? Epidemiologists study disease diffusion, which shares similarities to crime diffusion, but adopting concepts from other fields must occur with caution to prevent distortion or confusion.

This section will discuss three key concepts developed in the field of epidemiology, each of which can also be found in recent criminological literature. These concepts are: *contagion, epidemic,* and *diffusion.* I will begin by examining the contagion concept.

Exploring Contagion Effects

One of the key factors to uncovering an epidemic of disease is learning about the pathogen responsible for the disease outbreak. Is it a virus, a bacterium, or some other microorganism? In other words: what was the contagion that lead to sickness or death? Of course, in the case of the diffusion of social phenomena, such as homicide, the variables may be more complex than the introduction of a virus that ultimately leads to a disease. Still, the idea that certain factors may be considered contagions has potential value as a useful analogy to the homicide epidemic. In fact, the concept of contagion in reference to social phenomena has been debated since the inception of the field of sociology. In this section I will discuss both classical and contemporary perspectives on the controversial concept of contagion

The Classical Roots of Contagion

An early debate between Emile Durkheim (1951[1897]) and Gabriel Tarde (1903) on the concept of imitation set the stage for careful consideration of the diffusion of behavior, including the contemplation of the contagion concept. In general, the context for this debate was the determination of appropriate subject matter for the emerging field of sociology. However, the dispute between these two classical social philosophers also helps to inform the present discussion on the diffusion of homicide rates by uncovering how the concepts of contagion and epidemic might be applied to social behavior.

Durkheim (1951[1897]) discusses contagion in the context of the imitation of suicide. In highlighting suicide clusters -situations in which several suicides occur in the same vicinity in quick succession- Durkheim concludes that: "The idea of suicide may undoubtedly be communicated by contagion" (131). Durkheim defines the contagion concept applied to social behavior:

> In pathological biology, a disease is called contagious when it rises wholly or mainly from the development of a germ introduced into the organism from outside. Inversely, in so far as this germ has been able to develop thanks only to the active cooperation of the field in which it has taken root, the term "contagion" becomes inexact (128).

Clearly for Durkheim the contagion concept applies exclusively to a "germ" that causes disease without a positive interacting influence from the affected organism. Similarly, Durkheim extends the idea that the contagion concept is not appropriate when applied to a "germ" that develops in conjunction with the surrounding environment to understanding social behavior with reference to a "moral contagion":

Likewise, for an act to be attributed to a moral contagion it is not enough that the idea be inspired by a similar act. Once introduced into the mind, it must automatically and of itself have become active. Then contagion really exists, because the external act is reproduced by itself, entering into us by way of a representation. Imitation likewise exists, since the new act is wholly itself by virtue of the model it copies. But if the impression upon us of the latter takes effect only through our consent and participation, contagion is only figuratively present and the figure is inexact (128).

Durkheim's distinction is an important consideration. He maintains that a proper definition of the social behavior we call contagion only include examples of automatic actions. Contagion does not arise from any rational cognitive process. Other scholars have competing definitions of the contagion concept.

When contemporary scholars such as Malcolm Gladwell (2000) discuss the concept of contagion, they often express the concept in a figurative manner. This usage does not connote an automatic response from an external stimulus, such as Durkheim discusses. Gladwell provides a prime example of diffusion using the adoption of a certain style of shoes. Durkheim indicates that in such a case the imitation is "the impulse which drives us to seek harmony with the society to which we belong, and, with this purpose, to adopt the ways of thought or action which surround us" (124). And for Durkheim, an example such as the adoption of modes of dress cannot be considered true contagion since it involves "reasonable, deliberate behavior" and not automatic reflex. The spread of crack and the increase in homicide rates is clearly not a case of automatic reflex to an external stimulus. Rather, both processes involve considerable levels of deliberate thought and behavior that may seem reasonable given the social context and range of options available to the actors.

For the purposes of this book, one of the most important notions emphasized in Durkheim's discussion of the diffusion of behavior is his commentary on moral epidemics:

Finally, it would perhaps be interesting, to make the terminology precise, to distinguish moral epidemics from moral contagions; these two words are used carelessly for one another actually denote two very different sorts of things. An epidemic is a social fact, produced by social causes; contagion consists only in more or less repeated repercussions of individual phenomena (132).

The purpose of this book is to consider systematically the social causes that influenced key characteristics of the diffusion of the "social fact" of the homicide epidemic. Unfortunately, Durkheim makes his reference to moral epidemics in passing and does not discuss his ideas about moral epidemics in greater detail. However, Durkheim's recognition of the existence of "moral epidemics" demonstrates that the study of rapid changes in the rates of behavior has roots in classical social theory.

Ultimately, Durkheim dismisses the notion that imitation and contagion are important contributors to changes in suicide rates and the diffusion of other behaviors. However, Tarde, Durkheim's contemporary, argues that imitation does play an important role in the diffusion of behavior. A key portion of the dispute between Durkheim and Tarde is their disparate positions on the appropriate subject matter for sociology.

Durkheim's position is that the field of sociology should focus on "social facts." For Durkheim social facts are greater than the sum of individual actions and must be considered not in reference to individual processes but to other social facts. Tarde, on the other hand, views individual actions as biologists view cells in relation to organisms. For Tarde, social facts are simply an additive accumulation of individual actions.

Tarde (1903) discusses his approach to understanding the diffusion of behavior in his work on the "laws of imitation." His social psychological perspective views the adoption of new modes of behavior as the result of individual psychological processes:

This progress from within to without, if we try to express it more precisely, means two things: (1) That imitation of ideas precedes the imitation of their expression. (2) That imitation of ends precedes imitation of means. Ends or ideas are the inner things, means or expressions, the outer. Of course, we are led to copy from others everything which seems to us a new means for attaining our old ends, or satisfying our old wants, or a new expression for our old ideas; and we do this at the same time that we begin to adopt innovations which awaken new ideas and new ends in us. Only these new ends, these needs for novel kinds of consumption, take hold of us and propagate themselves in us much more readily and rapidly than the aforesaid means or expressions (186-187).

Evidently, Tarde's concept of imitation is quite different from Durkheim's. While Tarde views imitation as a psychological process that involves exposure to and the thoughtful adoption of innovations, Durkheim only considers actions that are automatic and without consideration to be true acts of imitation. Durkheim closely links the concepts of contagion and imitation, while Tarde views processes of imitation quite differently, indicating a process that involves reasoning and thoughtful interaction with new ideas.

The debate between Durkheim and Tarde highlights important points for this book. First, the term "contagion" with reference to a phenomenon such as homicide must be defined carefully. For example, when I discuss the contagious nature of the spread of crack cocaine that is linked to the increase in homicide rates across the U.S. and through major American cities, I am not implying a process of automatic response to stimuli following Durkheim's definition. Instead, I use the term "contagion" figuratively to depict the relationship between crack and homicide.

Tarde's social-psychological process may be involved in the diffusion of both crack and homicide, but this book does not focus on these processes. Instead, following Durkheim's contention that "moral epidemics" are best explained with reference to "social facts," I test the roles of the most important social variables that are associated with the homicide rate changes during the epidemic period and their effect on the presence, magnitude, and duration of the epidemic within major cities.

Deconstructing the Homicide Epidemic

The dramatic increase in youth homicide rates during the homicide epidemic was a public health crisis that defied the conventional wisdom on the prediction of trend changes. An essay on youth violence states: "...the volatility of youth-violence rates makes predictions of any sort highly uncertain. The run-up has been more akin to an outbreak of some contagious disease than to a conventional secular trend" (Cook and Laub 1998, 28). The seemingly contagious nature of homicide rate increases is also linked to another diffusion process that is akin to the spread of a contagious disease: the crack cocaine epidemic of the 1980s.

The dominant theory for explaining the recent homicide epidemic period is the relationship between crack cocaine and homicide (Blumstein 1995). Blumstein's theory can be summarized with the following set of statements:

1.   Drug dealers recruited young minority males to sell crack cocaine in urban areas in the 1980s.

2.   Young drug dealers armed themselves for self-protection.

3.   As more youth armed themselves, they developed an arms race.

4.   Youth resolved disputed with guns.

5.   More frequent use of firearms to resolve disputes lead to higher homicide rates in urban areas.

Although Blumstein does not state his theory in this fashion, these interrelated statements can be distilled from his thesis on the relationship between the crack epidemic and the homicide epidemic.

Blumstein proposes that homicide rates increased across the country following closely on the heels of the spread of crack cocaine. As drug dealers introduced crack into new markets, they recruited young males, especially young black males, to sell the drug. Drug dealers needed to find ways to resolve disputes, and for obvious reasons official channels of social control were unavailable. Guns presented a pragmatic technological solution: a young male could insure some level of respect and deter thieves with little physical effort.

Following Blumstein's thesis, as drug dealers in the late 1980s and early 1990s increasingly relied upon firearms for status and protection, they helped to create a more lethal environment. Other urban residents-even those not directly involved in the drug trade-also armed themselves in response to the more dangerous social context. This widespread increase in access to firearms resulted in a drastic increase in deaths from firearms.

Blumstein's theory suggests that the spread of crack through American cities can be considered a contagion that ultimately lead to the homicide epidemic. Furthermore, handguns can also be considered a contagion that lead to the homicide epidemic since the diffusion of firearms through populations of young urban males lead to an increase in fatalities.

Blumstein's theory remains the dominant theory on the recent homicide epidemic (Ousey and Lee 2002), and significant empirical evidence supports this theory. (e.g., Baumer 1994, Baumer et al. 1998, Cork 1999, Fox and Levin 2000). While this theory remains an important contribution to uncovering the dramatic increase in homicide rates during the epidemic period, one might question why this specific drug is so closely identified with homicide rate increase.

What are the characteristics of crack cocaine and the marketing of this drug that link crack to the homicide epidemic? Research indicates that American drug markets in general are commonly associated with violence for a variety of reasons (Goldstein 1985). Goldstein provides a widely cited description of the connection between drugs and violence in urban areas.

Goldstein's (1985) taxonomy indicates three major types of violence associated with drugs:

1. Psychopharmacological violence. Drug use may lead directly to irrational behavior, including violent behavior (494-495).

2. Economic compulsive violence. Drug users may commit crimes to secure money to purchase drugs (496).

3. Systemic violence. Drug dealers and users rely on violent measures to settle disputes and to protect themselves from robbery (496-502).

Although a weakness of this schema is that the categories are not mutually exclusive, it still provides a useful instrument for understanding the link between drugs and violence. The last of Goldstein's categories has received the most attention in connecting crack and homicide (e.g., Blumstein 1995, Ousey and Lee 2002). Blumstein highlights the "arms race" associated with the spread of crack, which relates directly to this systemic violence.

Goldstein connects crack to still other categories. Crack engenders violence over money matters, as evidenced by the concurrent rise in robberies and homicides (Blumstein 2000). Crack consumers with limited resources from legitimate work need to find ways to fund their habit. Although one available avenue is the role of user-dealer, funding the habit through the profit of drug sales, robbery also offers a viable alternative. While some evidence demonstrates that crack consumption breeds some level of psychopharmacological violence, macro-level research in the tradition followed in this book explores the relationship between drugs and violence by focusing on the systematic violence category.

An economic perspective is one approach to understanding the nature of the impact of crack cocaine on violence (see e.g., Grogger 2000, Grogger and Willis 2000). From the perspective of the marketplace, crack is simply a refinement of a product that had already received some level of popularity among segments of the American population.

Cocaine has a long history of use in the United States from early medicinal forms (and a key ingredient and name sake for Coca Cola) to more common recreational use in more recent decades (although cocaine and some of its derivatives are still available by prescription for pain relief). Before the advent of crack only the wealthy could afford cocaine.

The introduction of crack cocaine in the mid-1980s opened a new market for recreational cocaine usage. Crack can be sold and consumed in relatively small amounts, costing as little as five or ten dollars, which means that even indigent Americans can afford to use it. Furthermore, crack is an ideal product for promoting demand, because the euphoric high produced by crack consumption lasts only a short period of time, and hard-core users may consume the drug numerous times a day (Mieczkowski 1990). Some evidence demonstrates when a user smokes cocaine the drug is more addictive than when it is snorted or injected (Cone 1995).

The manufacture of crack is also a relatively simple process. The process requires only four basic ingredients: cocaine, baking soda (sodium bicarbonate), water, and a source of intense heat. A U.S. Park Police drug-enforcement officer from Washington, D.C., reports, "All it takes is twenty minutes in the microwave." (Cooper 1990, 41). Despite the relative ease of production, crack use has been mainly confined to major metropolitan areas (Belenko 1993).

Blumstein's (1995) theory on the connection between crack and homicide is logical considering the unique nature of crack cocaine. Crack can be easily manufactured, is affordable by those with low incomes, and can be consumed with great frequency. Qualitative research indicates that urban residents with few legitimate job prospects can make money and support their own habits through the sale of crack (see e.g., Bourgois 1996). Furthermore, high rates of usage and low dosage purchases could have lead to the kind of systemic violence indicated by Goldstein (1985). Finally, areas of severe resource deprivation, such as those found in many inner city areas in the U.S., have restricted access to social control mechanisms that can help prevent the sort of open market drug bazaar that is associated with the sale of crack. If one accepts that the emergence of crack markets lead to increased presence of firearms, which lead to an increase in deadly disputes, then the characteristics of crack cocaine and the crack market support the notion that crack can be viewed as a contagion (at least in a figurative sense). As the crack market spread through major cities throughout the U.S., the homicide rate increases followed.

Was crack cocaine a contagion that lead to the homicide epidemic? Because crack is a cheap derivative of cocaine, one would guess that the former would follow the same distribution route as the latter. Farmers grow coca, the plant from which cocaine is derived, in the Andean region of South America. The leaves must be chemically refined and then transported in the form of powdered cocaine to consumer nations such as the United States.

According to the National Drug Intelligence Center (NDIC) major cocaine distribution routes connect Mexico to El Paso and Los Angeles (2001). Los Angeles, in turn is connected to other major distribution hubs including Chicago, Detroit, and New York City. Miami also serves as a direct route to New York City. The NDIC identifies El Paso, Los Angeles, Houston, Miami, and cities in central Arizona as cocaine transportation hubs that supply cocaine to major American cities across the country. Figure 1 indicates the major cocaine hubs. The prominence of the East and West coasts is clearly evident, which is consistent with Blumstein's (1995) assertion that the homicide epidemic began in these areas after the introduction of crack cocaine.

Figure 1. Map of major hubs in the continental U.S.

Major U.S. cities are at the first levels of cocaine distribution and destination routes. These cities most likely experienced the earliest emergence of crack markets. Blumstein (1995) indicates that increased levels of violence followed the emergence of drug markets. Therefore, the diffusion of the flow of cocaine, the raw material needed for the production of crack cocaine, is likely the same path as the diffusion of increased levels of violence. The city-level research approach taken in this book allows for tests of whether or not changes in the homicide rates of major U.S. cities followed the route of cocaine through the country. If Blumstein is correct about the close relationship between the geographic distribution of crack and the diffusion of homicide rate increase, then cities along the cocaine route should follow a temporal pattern in rate changes tied to their geographic location along the route.

Blumstein highlights New York City and Los Angeles as two cities that began the epidemic, a pattern that could be predicted from the cocaine routes cited by the NDIC (2001). However, I go beyond considering a small group of major cities to look at the parameters of the epidemic for a larger population of cities. The geographical portion of this book should help uncover why some cities did not experience the epidemic at all. For example, a measure of the distance between primary cocaine supply cities and secondary cites could help determine the likelihood of the homicide epidemic presence. I also include a measure of the number of cocaine hubs within 500 miles of a city to account for the concentration of cocaine supply cities.

Very likely key social variables played a role in the geographical spread of the homicide epidemic along the location of the cocaine supply routes. Cities with higher poverty rates, for example, may have been more likely to experience the homicide epidemic. Cities may have also been more susceptible to the homicide epidemic because of their population size and proportion of young minorities. These variables may have interacted with the introduction of crack to create a deadly mix. The notion of "contingent causation," the idea that the violence produced by drug markets is contingent upon preexisting variables associated with violence, is discussed in greater detail later in this chapter when I discuss the overarching theoretical framework used in this book. The next section discusses the concept of "epidemic" in reference to the increase in homicide rates.

Defining a Homicide Epidemic

As mentioned in the previous chapter, the epidemic concept used by epidemiologists is defined as an "unusually high incidence of a disease where 'unusually high' is fixed in time, in space, and in the persons afflicted as compared with previous experience" (Hagget 2000, 2). This definition, although not explicitly cited by criminologists, seems to fit the intended purpose in analyzing the recent homicide epidemic. One of the very few examples of criminologists using the epidemic concept occurs in Moore and Tonry's (1998) exploration of youth violence:

Consider, finally, the word "epidemic." The public health community has brought this word into common usage. But when public health specialists use the word, they have a specific technical meaning in mind. They mean that a particular health problem (in this case, injury caused by violence) is above the expected level. The expectation could have been set by past trends, or by past trends within particular demographic groups, or by past trends within population groups possessing certain "risk factors" for the health condition. Thus an epidemic of youth violence means nothing more than that more trauma is inflicted by violent episodes in the youth population than in the past (5).

Both the epidemiological definition of the term "epidemic" and Moore and Tonry's discussion clarify that experts define an epidemic by the relative difference between expectations based on trends and unexpected increases. Another, more refined, definition from a standard handbook on communicable diseases defines the concept as:

> The occurrence in a community or region of cases of an illness (or an outbreak) clearly in excess of expectancy. The number of cases indicating presence of an epidemic will vary according to the infectious agent, size and type of population exposed, previous experience or lack of exposure to the diseases, and time and place of occurrence; epidemicity is thus relative to usual frequency of disease in the same area, among the specified population, at the same season of the year (Benenson 1990).

This definition of an epidemic provides clear guidelines for the appropriate application of the technical term *epidemic*. Although homicide is not an illness or disease, an increase in homicide rates falls under these guidelines when the rate is in excess of expectancy. The difficulty in applying the term *epidemic* is that the phenomenon under consideration must be "clearly in excess of expectancy." Exactly when a phenomenon reaches a point clearly in excess of expectancy is not always obvious and requires careful analysis of rate trends. Scholars who adopt the term *epidemic* must state their operational definition unambiguously so that the sorts of trends that fall into this category are clear.

How can it be determined when homicide rates are "clearly in excess of expectancy?" Comparing rates over time is the only way to identify if an epidemic occurred. No one can predict future homicide rates, but historical trends can indicate when rates increased more quickly and to greater heights than would be expected based on general trends. The period of the late 1980s and early 1990s in the U.S. is clearly one of interest. According to the Department of Justice, between 1985 and 1991 the national homicide rate increased by 25 percent. Furthermore, the national rate of 10.5 per 100,000 people in 1991 is the second highest homicide rate in a century. Prior to the homicide trend increase that began in 1985, the national rate trend was declining. Between 1980 and 1985, the rate had fallen by 22 percent.

A drastic decline followed the incline of the late 1980s and early 1990s. In fact, between 1991 and 2000 the national homicide rate fell by 42 percent. The dramatic incline of homicide trends during the late 1980s and early 1990s marks a clear case that meets the technical definition of an epidemic. The burgeoning homicide rate of the late 1980s was a rare event in that century. A homicide rate as high as the rate that peaked during the early 1990s is relatively unusual. The unusually high homicide rate trend identifies the epidemic period. I discuss the technical definition used to determine if and when individual cities experienced an epidemic in detail in chapter 4.

An important characteristic of the epidemiological definition of disease cited above is that epidemicity is relative to the usual frequency of diseases in a specified population. This point that certain populations may be affected to a much greater degree than others is highly relevant to the study of the most recent homicide epidemic.

Disaggregating the national homicide rate by age, race, and gender demonstrates the importance of considering the particular social groups that are most affected by the increase in rates. I review the empirical research on the homicide epidemic in greater detail in the next chapter, but a brief preview here underscores the value of disaggregating rates by different groups.

The homicide epidemic affected the youth to the greatest degree. The greatest increase in homicide rates was for people between the ages of 14 and 24. Homicide rates increased for both black and white males as well as black females. However, young black males experienced levels of violence that far surpassed all other groups. For example, according to the Department of Justice, during the epidemic period the national rate of homicide victimization for white males between the ages 18 and 24 peaked around 18 per 100,000 people. Black males in the same age group peaked at an astonishing rate of 183. Based on these figures, if we adopt the notion that epidemicity is relative to the frequency of diseases in a specified population the definition of the term *homicide epidemic* applies to some extent to youth in general (although white females did not experience an increase during this period), and most certainly to young black males.

The nominal definition of *homicide epidemic* for this book is: *The occurrence within a territorial unit, such as a nation or city, of cases of homicide clearly in excess of expectancy.* This definition is important in identifying the period of national homicide rate increases that took place in the late 1980s and early 1990s as an epidemic. During this period the national homicide rate increased quickly to a high level, clearly in excess of expectancy.

How similar are social epidemics, such as the diffusion of homicide rates, to epidemics of disease? Gladwell (2000) discusses the ways in which social epidemics mimic epidemics of disease. Gladwell cites three important characteristics associated with epidemics. These characteristics include:

1. Stickiness. A phenomenon that becomes an epidemic must have what Gladwell calls "stickiness." Stickiness means something unique about the characteristics of the disease or phenomenon makes it take hold or become popularly adopted.

2. The power of the few. Gladwell points out that in cases of the diffusion of both disease and product adoption, a small number of innovators influence many adopters.

3. The power of context. A key aspect of Gladwell's taxonomy is the importance of the context in which diffusion processes operate. Ultimately the environment surrounding the diffusion processes help to determine the extent of adoption or infection.

These characteristics apply to the homicide epidemic, which has been attributed to the spread of handguns. For example, the stickiness factor is related to the both the highly addictive nature of crack and the unique nature of deadly violence.

Fear of strangers and of gun violence is an especially striking issue in urban areas (see e.g., Zimring and Hawkins 1997). Such fear can promote members of violence prone communities to arm themselves as Blumstein (1995) suggests. The power of the few is related the idea that a few highly violent community members can create hyper-violent atmosphere. Finally, the power of context can be related to the social characteristics of the urban environment in which homicide rates increased during the epidemic. Preexisting conditions such as poverty could influence an increased reliance on guns for protection, since other forms of dispute resolution, such as calling police, appear inadequate. The power of context is of importance to this book since I focus on social variables that influenced key parameters of the diffusion of the homicide epidemic within major American cities.

The Role of Contingent Causation

The theory of contingent causation is one of the most important theoretical extensions of Blumstein's theory (Zimring and Hawkins 1997). Zimring and Hawkins echo Gladwell's (2000) assertion that social context is key to the diffusion of social phenomenon such as homicide rates. In contrast to scholars who highlight an "inevitable" connection between drugs and violence, Zimring and Hawkins point out:

> In predicting the impact of illegal markets on rates of homicide, the contingencies about the type of product involved, the people who buy and sell it, and the larger social environment in which this commerce takes place are more important than the bare facts of illegal commerce. Little is presently known about the specific conditions that promote violence in drug markets. One reason that little is known about the specific conditions that promote violence is that unjustified generalizations about the inevitable connection between violence and illegality have been the conventional wisdom about drugs in the United States (153).

Zimring and Hawkins' developed their theory to account for international differences in the relationship between illegal drug markets and violence. Studies in major American cities, such as New York City, Washington, D. C., and Detroit, have consistently found a strong correlation between illegal drug markets and violence. However, investigations in major cities in European nations, such as the Netherlands and Italy, do not find this correlation.

Zimring and Hawkins hypothesize that "the creation and expansion of illegal markets will produce extra homicides when social circumstances conducive to lethal violence already exist" (153). The likelihood of increased violence is associated with a drug market, such as the crack cocaine market, contingent upon the specific qualities of the drug and the social circumstances present in the marketplace. Therefore, the systemic violence that is associated with drug markets is not simply a product of the introduction of drugs. Instead the violence depends on key contingencies.

What explains the difference in homicide rates between American and European cities? Following Zimring and Hawkins' theory of contingent causation, the high levels of drug-related homicide in American urban centers compared to the low rates found in Europe can be accounted for in part because major American cities have a higher baseline of characteristics associated with violence.

One of the problems with this theory is that Zimring and Hawkins do not explicitly state what "contingencies" are responsible for increased violence; however, the general logic may prove useful in explaining why some cities in the United States may have been more susceptible to the homicide epidemic than others. Their general logic may also explain variations in the magnitude and duration of the epidemic period. Their hypothesis that "extra homicides" are the result of social context indicates that cities with the highest levels of social variables associated with violence are the most likely to experience increases in violence following the introduction of a new drug market. Therefore, cities with such characteristics are more likely to experience a homicide epidemic. Such cities are also at greater risk for experiencing an epidemic of greater magnitude and longer duration. This assertion is valuable for explaining, for example, why cities might vary in their susceptibility to the homicide epidemic, despite the common presence of a crack cocaine market.

One of the goals of this book is to uncover the role of "social circumstances conducive to lethal violence" in affecting the drastic increase in homicide rates associated with the homicide epidemic. The hypotheses tested should reveal the extent to which social variables associated with violence affected why cities experienced homicide rate increases of varied magnitude and duration.

The End of the Epidemic

The sharp increase in homicide rate trends in the late 1980s and early 1990s confounds criminologists because explaining a rapid increase in crime rates with theories that focus entirely on social structural variables that change more slowly is difficult. Social variables may play an important role in explaining city-level variation in the homicide epidemic parameters, but they do not, by themselves, explain the emergence of the epidemic.

The sharp decline in homicide rates has also drawn interest because of the rapidity of change, and the decline also "remains something of a puzzle" (Rosenfeld 2002: 25). Scholars continue to focus on the end of the epidemic period and the declining rates that followed (see e.g., Blumstein and Wallman 2000, Conklin 2003).

The variables that influenced the end of the epidemic period are important considerations for two of the epidemic parameters that I analyze in this book: magnitude and duration. The same social variables may have affected both of these parameters, although the variables may have affected these two parameters to different degrees.

Independent Variables

Counteracting the Homicide Epidemic with Police

Bolstering the police force was a major strategy to combat the burgeoning homicide rate increases. Criminologists cite the main contributions of policing:

1. Police tactics. Theories that link policing techniques to decreased levels of criminal activity, such as the broken windows theory, indicate that changing policing techniques can affect crime rates including homicide (see e.g., Wilson and Kelling 1982). Generally, experts argue that simply expanding the size of the police force within a city can ameliorate crime rates (e.g., Levitt 2004).

2. Drug law enforcement. Increasing penalties for drug-related crimes and increasing police focus on drug crimes can remove offenders who are more likely to become violent offenders. The incarceration of drug dealers also makes them unavailable as potential targets of homicide as well. Drug law enforcement also increases the costs of using and dealing drugs, a deterrent for such behavior. Increasing costs can reduce the number of people involved in disputes surrounding the drug trade and thereby decrease levels of violence. Of course, police enforcement contributes to the destabilization of drug markets as actors are incarcerated and released, which could actually exacerbate violence. Additionally, a cost-benefit analysis demonstrates that from a market perspective

policing makes illegal drugs more expensive and profitable, possibly increasing the incentive to sell the drugs.

3. Gun law enforcement. Increasing penalties for gun-related crimes and increasing policing of firearms can remove offenders from the population and deter other prospective offenders from carrying firearms. A decrease in the number of armed citizens could lead to a decline in deadly violence.

4. Incarceration rates. Prison expansion increased rapidly during the period of the homicide epidemic. The removal of violent criminals could decrease levels of violent crime because the capacity to commit violent crimes is severely restricted in the prison setting. The community could also experience a general deterrence effect when users and dealers outside of prison learn that police have incarnated community members. Of course, the value of incarceration, especially for non-violent offenders, must be weighed against the costs to society of removing people for long periods and creating feelings of institutional distrust among affected groups.

I discuss the research on each of these four areas in the next chapter. Next, I move to the strength of the economy, a frequently cited factor in declining crime rates.

The Effect of the Economy on the Homicide Epidemic

Economic variables are often mentioned as predictors of crime rate trends. Offenders contribute to both the legitimate and illicit economies. Increasing wages and employment opportunities could lead potential offenders away from the black market. Positive economic changes could lead to fewer shootings. An improving economy should reduce the number of probable offenders and victims, as legitimate work becomes a more attractive alternative to illegitimate occupations.

The Effect of Demography on the Homicide Epidemic

I already noted that the homicide epidemic was narrowly channeled demographically. Changes to the demographic structures of cities could have an impact on the homicide rate. A decline in the populations most likely to become offenders or victims reduces crime. For example, if the share of young people (the group most likely to contribute to homicide rates during the epidemic period) declined, then homicide rates would also decline.

Theoretical Expectations for the Homicide Epidemic

What is the theoretical framework guiding this book? I derive a series of hypotheses from Blumstein's theory (1995) and the contingent causation extension from Zimring and Hawkins (1997). More generally, overarching theoretical questions include: did the variables that affected the homicide parameters have the same effect on each parameter? Or did the effects of variables differ by parameter? The same variables that affected whether or not a city experienced an epidemic may not have had the same explanatory strength for the magnitude or duration. For example, law enforcement tactics may affect the duration of the epidemic period, but have no affect on the presence of an epidemic, since policing is largely reactive to crime and social concerns and not preventative. The next sections discuss the specific hypotheses for each of the epidemic parameters.

Explaining the Presence of the Epidemic

Why did some cities experience the epidemic period, while other cities did not? Fundamental social variables should help to uncover the answer to this question. One of the most important variables affecting whether or not cities experienced an epidemic at all during the national homicide epidemic period is the population size and population density of individual cities. In this chapter I have discussed the theoretical arguments, drawn especially from Blumstein, that indicate the importance of this variable. Concerning the spread of crack cocaine, the largest cities were the first to experience growth in this drug market, and if homicide rates trends followed the diffusion of crack, then the largest and most densely populated cities would be more likely to have a homicide epidemic.

Another important variable that could affect whether a city experienced the epidemic or not includes the percent of black youth and the age-structure of cities (i.e., the relative size of the youth cohort), since scholars hypothesize that young, black males had the greatest involvement with crack cocaine. Cities with a smaller percent of black males and smaller youth cohorts would be less likely to experience an epidemic since they would likely have a relatively smaller population of participants in the crack market.

Of course, race considered alone has no theoretical value in this instance. However, the interaction between race and other social factors is important. I also consider family structure. Family structure may not affect the likelihood of an epidemic to the same degree as population size, and density, and the proportion of likely crack market participants. However, variables such as the percent of female-headed households could indicate a lack of family and community cohesion that leads to less supervision of youth. A larger proportion of unsupervised youth would likely increase the number of young people who could engage in deviant activities, including participation in the drug trade that is linked to higher homicide rates.

Finally, the poverty level may also play an important role in determining which cities experienced the epidemic. Concentrations of poverty are tied to a weakening of "collective efficacy," which leads to a reduction in the control of illicit behavior in public (see e.g., Sampson and Raudenbush 1997). Poverty adds to the problems of supervising illicit behavior, and increases the likelihood that illicit opportunities for making money such as dealing drugs are more attractive. Furthermore, the high concentration of poverty in many cities could also increase the likelihood that people would seek the self-medicalization and euphoria provided by drugs such as crack cocaine.

I have outlined the social variables that seem to have the greatest affect on rates of violence; however, the violence associated with these variables is also the focus of many public policy decisions. For example, increasing the number of police may prevent violence. Policing is the only variable discussed here that can be rapidly changed in response to changes in crime trends. A high number of police in a city may have protected that city from experiencing a homicide epidemic.

Explaining the Magnitude of the Epidemic

Why did some cities experience an epidemic period of greater magnitude than others? If policing affects crime rates, then policing should have strongly affected the magnitude of the epidemic. A well-organized police force could counter crime rates and decrease the negative impact of rate changes. Policing has the greatest potential of all the variables discussed in this section to reduce the magnitude of the epidemic. Policing can remove potential offenders from the population and deter the remaining population from participation in illicit behavior.

Demographic structures of cities also may have played a role in the magnitude of the epidemic. A greater population size and density would likely have lead to a greater magnitude. A relatively large proportion of youth would likely have increased the magnitude. High levels of poverty and unemployment, especially in conjunction with high populations of minority residents, could also have increased the magnitude of the homicide epidemic. The concentration of these variables lowers the level of supervision of illicit behavior, and desperate circumstances make participation in the illicit economy a more likely alternative to the legitimate labor market.

Explaining the Duration of the Epidemic

Why did the length of the epidemic period vary by city? The variables linked to the duration of the epidemic period are most likely the same list as those tied to magnitude, although some important shifts in the strength of the relationship could have occurred. Policing is likely to have the greatest impact on the duration, for the same reasons discussed for the magnitude of the epidemic. However, economic variables may have also had a strong impact on duration. Since policing increases the costs of participation in illicit behavior, policing may interact with economic variables such as unemployment and poverty. For example, offenders may have been more likely to continue the pursuit of risky behaviors in spite of the increased costs brought about by policing in cities where unemployment and poverty are highest. On the other hand, potential offenders may be more likely to join the legitimate labor market when economic tides improve.

The demographic structure of cities may also have contributed to the duration of the epidemic period, although economic and policing factors probably played a more vital role in the duration of the epidemic.

Chapter Summary

Blumstein's (1995) theory on the relationship between crack cocaine and the homicide epidemic is the dominant theory used to explain the epidemic of the late 1980s and early 1990s. Key concepts associated with this framework include epidemic, contagion, and diffusion.

Identifying and clarifying these concepts are important steps in moving toward a theoretical framework that informs the study of the city-level variations in the presence, magnitude, and duration of the epidemic period. How concepts like "epidemic" apply to homicide rate increases is central to explaining the operation of homicide rate changes.

Zimring and Hawkins (1997) argue that rates of violence will be greater when drug markets are introduced in areas with characteristics associated with violence. Although this hypothesis has received some support, it has not been tested on the magnitude and duration of the homicide epidemic. Furthermore, the role of policing on these two parameters should be included the model, since policing has the potential to greatly impact these characteristics. Finally, I consider the effects of economic and social variables on the epidemic parameters.

The next chapter will review the research on the most recent homicide epidemic and the social characteristics associated with violence in urban areas. The chapter will conclude with a series of formally stated hypotheses that will be tested in this study.

CHAPTER 3

What We Know about the Homicide Epidemic and Where We Go From Here

Criminologists are intrigued by the national homicide epidemic that occurred in the late 1980s and early 1990s, and their research has revealed some important findings. The correlation between the influx of crack cocaine and the increase in homicide rates has generated significant interest. Although research continues to provide support for Blumstein's (1995) theory in general and also for many of the specific hypotheses suggested by his work, the nature of important attributes of the diffusion process, such as the presence, magnitude, and duration, associated with the epidemic are still not well understood.

This chapter will review the extant literature on the homicide epidemic period. First, I will discuss the structure of the U.S. national homicide rate. Next, I will discuss the research that relates directly to hypotheses drawn from Blumstein's theory on the relationship between crack cocaine and the homicide epidemic. Finally, I will review the variables that have demonstrated the most salience in the epidemic period.

I will test these variables to determine their role in creating a fertile social environment to prompt a homicide epidemic. Specifically, I will test these variables to determine if they are positively related to the presence, magnitude, and duration of the homicide epidemic. Finally, based on the review of literature on the specific causes of the homicide epidemic and the review of research on homicide rates, I will present a series of specific hypotheses that will be tested in this book.

The Structure the National Homicide Rate Trend

One of the debates concerning the homicide epidemic period is whether or not the homicide rate follows a pattern that can be properly termed contagious. Some crime experts suggest an exponential growth rate, also known as "tipping point" theory (e.g., La Free 1999, Gladwell 2000, Jones and Jones 2000).

A "tipping point" refers to the point at which a trend changes from a few cases and to a sharp increase in cases. Tipping point theory indicates that once the sharp increase occurs the process becomes self-generating. Some experts highlight the homicide trends in the late 1980s and early 1990s as an epidemic period since the rate increased so dramatically.

McDowall (2002) questions the accuracy of tipping point theory as an explanation for the national homicide rate trend of the United States. Specifically, McDowell tested the national rate trend for nonlinear structures, including the kind of exponential rate changes suggested by tipping point theory. McDowall uses a number of statistical tests to determine if the national homicide rate trend is non-linear. Contrary to the suggestions of tipping point theory, McDowall found that the homicide rate trend for the United States is linear. This finding is informative for the national homicide rate, but cannot be extended to the city level.

The longitudinal homicide rates for individual cities within the United States follow a wide array of patterns, not all of which are linear (Messner et al. 2005). While McDowall refutes the tipping point model for the national homicide rate during the epidemic period, this finding neither negates the utility of an epidemiological approach concerned with the diffusion of phenomena, nor does the finding address the non-linear patterns of many city-level homicide rate trends.

The next section will review the research engendered by Blumstein's (1995) theory that links the emergence of crack cocaine in urban areas to the increase in homicide rates.

The Homicide Epidemic and Crack Cocaine

Blumstein (1995) theorizes that the spread of crack cocaine into urban areas led to an increase in firearms and a subsequent increase in homicide rates. A number of studies have examined the relationship between crack cocaine and homicide and tested hypotheses drawn from this theory (e.g., Baumer 1994, Baumer et al. 1998, Cork 1999, Grogger 2000, Grogger and Willis 2000, Johnson, Golub and Dunlap 2000, Ousey and Lee 2002). This body of research has generally provided support for Blumstein's theory. This section will review the empirical tests that have evaluated the plausibility of Blumstein's specific hypotheses.

One approach to testing for a relationship between an increase in crack cocaine use and an increase in the homicide rate is to consider the timing of crack cocaine increases and the timing of the increase in homicide rates. If an increase in crack cocaine use preceded the increase in homicide rates, then these two variables may be positively related. Of course, researchers positing causal relations based on timing must always be cautious. However, the logical error of using a purely *post hoc ergo propter hoc* argument can be avoided by carefully analyzing the probable causes of the relationship.

Studies that look at the timing of the introduction of crack and the timing of the homicide rate epidemic rely on a number of different measures for determining the timing of the increase in crack use: Baumer (1994) relies on Drug Use Forecasting (DUF) data on positive drug tests; Cork (1999), Baumer et al (1998), and Ousey and Lee (2002) rely on the Federal Bureau of Investigation's Uniform Crime Report (UCR) data on arrests for the sale, manufacture, or possession of opium, cocaine, and cocaine derivatives; Grogger and Willis (2000) rely on a combination of surveys of police chiefs, congressional testimony from police officials, and the number of emergency room visits in metropolitan areas attributed to smoking cocaine. Although Messner, et al. (2005) looks more closely at the issue of city-level variation in the timing of the epidemic, this study includes no direct measure of cocaine.

Baumer (1994) used data on positive drug tests of arrestees and city-level crime data from the Uniform Crime Reporting (UCR) Program to test for a relationship between rates of cocaine use among arrestees and rates of homicide, robbery, and burglary. Baumer reported a significant positive relationship between cocaine use and robbery, a more modest effect on homicide rates, and no effect for burglary rates. While the modest effect of cocaine use on homicide rates provides only limited support for the hypothesis that crack cocaine and homicide rates are related, these findings must be considered with some caution.

First, as Baumer points out, the measures used in these tests rely on general data measures. While smoking crack can result in a positive test for cocaine, a positive test provides no indication of what form of cocaine the person consumed. Furthermore, the general homicide measure does not indicate what proportion of homicides can be attributed to the forms of homicide that are potentially related to violence associated with the crack market, such as gun-related homicides.

Second, this study relies on an average set of variable rates computed using rates from 1989-1991. Messner et al. (2003) evaluated the timing of the homicide epidemic in major cities in the U.S., and their research indicates that the homicide epidemic began and ended at different time periods for different cities, as suggested by Blumstein (1995). In fact, the period between 1989 and 1991 does mark a time when the last of the cities began the homicide epidemic and the first cities began the decline in homicide rates following the epidemic. However, what is not clear is if the average homicide rates of for this transitional period accurately reflect the longitudinal relationship between crack cocaine and the homicide epidemic.

Grogger and Willis (2000) rely primarily on a survey of police chiefs and emergency room admissions for drug-related emergencies to test for a relationship between the growth of crack use and an increase in urban crime rates. Grogger and Willis use a counterfactual approach to the problem. Instead of looking directly at homicide rate increases in urban areas, Grogger and Willis begin by looking at suburban areas that did not experience the homicide epidemic. They ask: how much lower would crime rates be if crack had not appeared on the scene? The approach involves comparing rates of central city index crimes with the rates of these crimes in the suburbs of those cities before and after the introduction of crack. The advantage of this approach is that a researcher can determine the rate of "excess" crimes for central cities because the rate of crime change in the suburbs over the same time period provides an estimate of crime rate change due to factors other than crack.

The result of this test reveals that the increase in crack use had a positive effect on a number of index crimes, including homicide. Grogger and Willis report, "the difference-in-difference estimate for murder indicates that the arrival of crack caused murder rates to rise by 4.4 per 100,000 population, an amount equal to 19% of the before-crack murder rate in the central cities" (523). The notion that crack use and the associated violence associated is primarily concentrated in central cities is supported by this research, since the greatest changes in crime rates after the introduction of crack were evident in the central cities, while suburban areas experienced much lower increases.

Cork's (1999) research helps to highlight the mechanisms through which the growth of crack cocaine use increased urban homicide rates. Cork's work provides some of the strongest evidence supporting Blumstein's (1995) assertion that the spread of crack cocaine prompted an increase in firearm acquisition, which then lead to the increase in homicide rates in urban areas. Cork used city-level data to fit an innovation diffusion model to test the relationship between the spread of crack and also the increase in youth homicides due to firearms.

The statistical model anticipated in this case is one in which the rate of crack arrests and the rate of juvenile gun homicides followed a pattern of initial stability leading to a sharp increase and subsequent decline. The sharp increase and decrease are theorized to be a result of the diffusion of crack and youth gun homicide. Rates begin to increase as a small number of "innovators" adopt a phenomenon (e.g., crack use and firearms acquisition) and a steep incline in rates occurs as "imitators," a much larger population, follow suit and adopt the phenomenon as well. Eventually, the population of possible "adopters" becomes saturated and the rate of new adopters declines precipitously. At this point the rate of occurrence drops off.

Using this approach, Cork found that crack arrests did generally follow an innovation diffusion pattern. Furthermore, gun homicide among youth followed a similar pattern after the diffusion of crack. Cork found that the diffusion of crack into large American cities was followed by an increase in gun homicides among youth. This research provides support for Blumstein's (1995) hypothesis that the introduction of crack lead to the homicide epidemic.

Cork (1999) points out that the increase in gun-related homicides was primarily among juvenile offenders, the same group hypothesized to be the most likely to participate in the crack cocaine market. In fact, offenders older than 25 demonstrated no growth in gun-related homicide. Furthermore, non-gun homicides among juvenile offenders did not significantly increase during this period. These findings indicate that the national homicide increase during this period is due to youth gun homicides. Cork's results represent the most direct test of Blumstein's theory and provide significant support for the central hypotheses.

The Homicide Epidemic and Geography

Another key hypothesis proposed by Blumstein (1995) concerning the relationship between crack and homicide is that the diffusion process began in the coastal cities of the United States and then spread inward toward the Midwest. This hypothesis has not received the same degree of attention as the relationship between the timing of the influx of crack and the timing of the increase in homicide rates. However, a small number of studies have tested this hypothesis (e.g., Cork 1999, Messner et al. 2005). These studies lend general support for the coastal hypothesis.

Cork (1999) tested for spatial patterns in the homicide rate increases using cluster analysis to determine the accuracy of Blumstein's (1995) predictions that the increase in crack cocaine and the increase in homicide rates that followed began in the coastal regions. This prediction was confirmed. Cork reports that the crack rate increases began in clusters of cities first on the West Coast and in the Northeastern U.S. Gun homicide rate increases followed a similar pattern with clusters in Southern California and in the Northeast. The latest rate increases for both crack and gun homicide involved clusters in the Rustbelt and the South and in the Ozarks, areas more centrally located in the U.S.

Other research considers the city-level spatial dynamics of the homicide rate increases across the nation. Messner et al. (2003) examined the coastal hypothesis by considering the location of the vanguard cities of the homicide epidemic (those cities that first experienced the beginning and the end of the epidemic). Their findings demonstrate the role of the spatial component in the epidemic's diffusion. In general, cities in the country's coastal regions were the first to experience both the incline and decline in rates. Other non-coastal cities later followed the trends set by the vanguard cities[1].

The Social Context of the Epidemic

The previous section reviewed the extant literature on the relationship between crack cocaine and homicide rates. This research provides support for the hypothesis that the introduction of crack in urban areas lead to the increase in homicide rates. However, one of the purposes of this book is to ascertain why some cities experienced the homicide epidemic, while others did not. Additionally, this book seeks to ascertain how key variables influenced the magnitude and duration of the epidemic.

This section will provide a review of research on the key social structural variables that are related to the homicide epidemic. These variables begin with city-level characteristics such as city population size and density. The review of research continues with the specific social groups that were affected to the greatest degree by the homicide epidemic. This review will provide the basis for the series of hypothesis presented at the end of this chapter.

I do not hypothesize a causal relationship between social contextual variables and the homicide epidemic. I am not arguing that variables like city size or age structure are the direct cause of the homicide epidemic. Since an epidemic period lasts for only a relatively short period of time, it is unlikely that variables that undergo slow change such as city size and age structure are the direct cause of the epidemic. Rather, the goal of this book is to ascertain what kind of social structure creates inviting environment in which a homicide epidemic is more likely to occur. Furthermore, this book seeks to uncover the contributions of these variables to the magnitude and duration of the homicide epidemic.

Regardless of the direct cause of the homicide epidemic, the homicide rates in major American cities did not change in unison. The research discussed in the previous section indicates significant variation

---

[1] Vanguard cities are the cities that were first to experience the homicide epidemic incline or decline. Messner et al. 2005 use this term.

in the timing of the epidemic that varied both by the size of cities and their geographical location. This book seeks to build on this line of research by determining the kind of social environments that are positively related to the presence, magnitude, and duration of the homicide epidemic.

While cities that experienced the homicide epidemic varied in the timing for the incline and decline of the epidemic period, experts do not fully understand how social variables affected these important parameters of the homicide epidemic. The following sections discuss the key variables that pertain to these issues.

The Role of City Size and Density

Cities with large, dense populations have historically been associated with higher crime rates, including violent crime (e.g., Bailey 1984, Land et al. 1990, Messner 1982). As Palen (2005) points out "historically, high density (the number of people per acre, block or other geographical unit) and crowding (the number of people per room, usually in housing) have been cited as a cause of epidemics, contagion, crime, and moral degradation" (166).

Large populations allow both greater anonymity and opportunity to commit crimes, two important ingredients for violent crime. Experts frequently cite the population size of cities as an important variable in regard to the homicide epidemic, especially concerning the relationship between crack cocaine and violence. Large population centers offer a viable marketplace to sell crack, and a larger population makes policing the transfer of cocaine into the city more difficult. Of course, drug dealers and users are also subject to becoming victims themselves in the relatively more dangerous environment in large cities, which makes the individualized protection provided by guns more appealing.

Blumstein (2000) argues that city size played an important role in homicide rates during the epidemic, noting the proportion of homicides attributed to major cities:

> Although no other city has as large an effect as New York, the importance of the largest cities is reflected in the relative contribution they make to the total homicide picture. In 1996, ten cities (New York, Chicago, Los Angeles, Detroit, Philadelphia, Washington, New Orleans, Baltimore, Houston, Dallas, in order of decreasing numbers of homicides)

accounted for fully one quarter of all the nation's homicides. In contrast, in 1991, seven cities (New York, Los Angeles, Chicago, Detroit, Houston, Dallas, and Washington) were needed to account for a quarter of U.S. Homicides (36).

Blumstein (2000) also presents data on gun-related homicide rates and city populations. Blumstein's disaggregated his data into four population city size groups and the plotted patterns demonstrate that cities with populations over one million experienced homicide rate increases of the greatest magnitude. I will test the hypothesis that city size is related to the magnitude of the homicide epidemic more directly in this book using individual cities, rather than city groups, to test the relationship.

The Role of Age Structure

One of the strongest predictors of both homicide offending and victimization risk is age. Criminologists agree that aggregate rates of violent crime peak around the period between late teens and young adulthood and then decline thereafter. In the early 1980s experts argued that the age-crime curve is invariant over time (Hirshi and Gottfredson 1983). However, the literature exhibits considerable debate on this point. Some researchers argue that more refined measures of criminal activity reveal some degree of variance both across time and by specific offense (see e.g., Greenberg 1985 and Steffensmeier et al. 1989). Although this topic continues to generate debate, the fact remains that higher violent crime rates are associated with teenagers and young adults.

The variance in the age of homicide offenders during the period of the homicide epidemic has received a significant amount of attention from criminologists (e.g., Cook and Laub 1998, Bennet, DiIulio, and Walters 1996). Research on the homicide epidemic using rates disaggregated by age reveals that the increase in homicide rates was greatest among youthful offenders (Cook and Laub 1998, Cork 1999).

The proportional rate of homicide for both victims and offenders increased among youth during the epidemic. As Fox (2000) points out "age patterns are similar for victims and offenders, as most killings are intragenerational" (292). In the case of the homicide epidemic, the intragenerational nature of homicide has resulted in increases in youth rates, even while homicide rates decreased among Americans over the age of 25 (USDOJ 2004).

One theory on crime rate increase, including homicide rate increase, highlights the role of the age structure of a population: more youth means more violent crime. I review this explanation in the next section.

The Role of Cohort Size

One of the most intriguing demographic explanations for the variation in homicide rates is that some cohorts have a greater likelihood to commit deviant acts than others. This explanation indicates that larger cohorts are more likely to produce a higher proportion of deviants, including those who commit homicides. This approach is related to ideas drawn from the Easterlin (1978, 1987) hypothesis, which proposes that larger cohorts experience relative deprivation of resources (e.g., job opportunities).

The youth cohort size approach is interesting because it locates the source of crime increase with purely demographic measures. Simply put, a higher number of youth born into a particular cohort will produce more crime, compared to smaller cohorts. O'Brien et al. argue that the size of cohorts plays a key role in increases of homicide rates (1999). In fact, researchers who support the fundamental role of cohort characteristics in determining crime rates have criticized Blumstein's (1995) theory for its *ad hoc* nature, preferring a more general theory that accounts for longitudinal patterns in homicide rate change (O'Brien et al., 1999).

However, age structure has not proven a good predictor of crime rates for the period of the homicide epidemic. Predictions made about the decade of the 1980s indicated that crime rates would drop as a result of changes to the demographic structure that included the "aging out" of the offspring of the baby boomer cohort (e.g., Blumstein et al. 1980, Fox 1978). This predicted decline did not occur, and experts pointed to the crack epidemic as the cause of crime rate increases (Blumstein 1995), despite a seemingly more favorable demographic structure.

As Fox (2000) points out, homicide rates increased in the late 1980s and early 1990s at the same time that the proportion of the population in the age group most likely to contribute to increased rates was actually in decline. Homicide rates disproportionately increased among young teenagers and young adults, despite declining cohort sizes. This fact points to the need to find alternative explanations for the rate increases that move beyond a reliance solely on cohort characteristics to assess the importance of period effects.

While the explanation of cohort size provides an interesting alternative to explain homicide rates over time, a number of issues arise that should give criminologists pause concerning the application of this approach to the most recent homicide epidemic. In general, higher crime rates may be related to the size of the youth cohort. However, this explanation does not account for key aspects of the recent epidemic. This book seeks to answer such questions as: What social processes lead to an unpredicted increase in violent crime among younger populations? If the size of the youth population is the most important predictor of violent crime, why did cities experience the epidemic according to a geographical pattern? Additionally, and key to the goals of this book: Why did cities vary in their likelihood to experience a homicide epidemic and in the magnitude and duration of such an epidemic?

The Role of Race

Race is a key variable for understanding variation in homicide rates in the United States. For example, in the year 2000, blacks were six times more likely than whites to be victims of homicide, and blacks were also over seven times more likely than whites to commit homicide in the same year (USDOJ, 2004). The relationship between race and homicide rates is an important element of the homicide epidemic that took place in the late 1980s and early 1990s.

Between 1980 and 2000 white homicide rates remained relatively stable with the lowest rate in 2000 at 3.4 and the highest rate in 1980 at 6.7. Even for the ten year period of the epidemic, roughly 1985 to 1995, white homicide rate ranges only from a low of 4.9 in 1995 to a high of 5.7 in 1991 (USDOJ, 2004).

Black homicide rates, on the other hand, have undergone a much greater fluctuation. Between 1980 and 2000, black homicide rates ranged from a low of 32.8 in 1984 to a high of 50.4 in 1991 (USDOJ, 2004). Notice that these two years fall within the time period of the homicide epidemic. Interestingly, during the epidemic period, both black and white homicide rates peaked in 1991, and declined thereafter. The confluence of homicide rates suggests that the same process may affect homicide rates regardless of race, although to a different degree.

This study uses measures of race, family structure, and economic deprivation to test for the effects of resource deprivation on the presence, magnitude, and duration of the homicide epidemic in major cities. The next section discusses the role of resource deprivation in greater detail.

The Role of Resource Deprivation

Experts cite a number of "usual suspects" to explain homicide rates. One of the most important variables is resource deprivation. A wealth of research indicates a positive relationship between resource deprivation and homicide in general (e.g., Krivo and Peterson 1996, Land et al. 1990, Lee 2000, Morenoff and Sampson 1997, Ousey 1999, Parker and McCall 1999, Sampson 1987, Wilson 1987, 1996). Much of this research has focused on the role of concentrated disadvantage (poverty, percent black, residential segregation, etc.) in hindering the effective operation of social institutions and limiting social mobility.

Ousey and Lee (2002) have reported that socioeconomic conditions played an important role in within-city variation of drug market activity and homicide rates during the epidemic period. This study represents an important test of hypotheses drawn from Zimring and Hawkins (1997) theory on contingent causation. However, researchers have not yet thoroughly examined how poverty influenced homicide rates in the epidemic period. Characteristics of the epidemic such as variations in magnitude and duration have not been assessed at the city level.

Resource deprivation contributes to a social environment in which the spread of drugs, such as crack cocaine, and also of violence, such as the spread of homicide rates, will be more likely. I predict that cities with high levels of resource deprivation will be more vulnerable to the onset of the crack epidemic and, therefore, also to the accompanying homicide epidemic. Furthermore, I also predict that such cities will also be more likely to experience longer homicide epidemic periods because the social mechanisms that can counteract such an epidemic will not function effectively.

The Role of the Unemployment Rate

The unemployment rate[2] is another city-level characteristic that is frequently cited in the literature on homicide. Generally, research indicates inconsistent effects for the unemployment rate on homicide rates (Land et al., 1990). Land et al. find that unemployment usually does not have a significant effect on homicide rates. However, when unemployment is significant, the sign of the coefficient is negative. A negative relationship indicates that as the unemployment rate increases, homicide rates decrease. However, the nature of the homicide epidemic of the late 1980s and early 1990s may have translated into a stronger effect for unemployment. If the spread in the black market crack sales was the primary engine that drove the homicide rate increases, then cities with higher unemployment rates may have a higher proportion of likely participants in the black market.

The Role of Policing

The role of policing is widely cited as a major force counteracting the increasing crime rate trends of the late 1980s and early 1990s. To summarize the reasoning: policing tactics that focus on drug and gun-related arrests reduce the rate of violent crime. Changing the focus of policing to more aggressively arrest and incarcerate those involved with drugs and violence will effectively reduce the overall amount of crime and specifically prevent homicide. Furthermore, simply having a higher number of officers per capita gives city administrators and police chiefs greater flexibility in responding to violence and the criminogenic conditions that lead to violence.

Summary of Hypotheses

I test a series of hypotheses in this study based on the criminological literature I reviewed. I have arranged these hypotheses in three sections according to the dependent variable. The first section deals with the presence of the epidemic, the second with the magnitude, and the third with the duration of the epidemic. Although the expected relationships are the same, they are listed and tested individually.

---

[2] The unemployment rate is based on the percent of the total civilian labor force.

Additionally I test for interaction effects between the social variables in the best-fitting statistical models and the cocaine hub variables. The cocaine hub variables are the distance between each city and the nearest cocaine hub and the number of cocaine hubs within 500 miles. I test for an interaction between the cocaine hub variables and the social variables in the best-fitting models to see if the effect of the cocaine hub variables varied by the best predictor variables. Normally, interaction effects are predicted directly from the theory guiding the research. However, in this case, the specific interaction effects are not clearly identified by the theoretical framework. Which social variables significantly affected the presence, magnitude, and duration of the epidemic is not apparent. The most probable significant interaction effects cannot be predicted without first determining which social variables influenced the parameters. I use the standard practice of relying on computed product terms to test for interaction effects.

Hypotheses on the Presence of the Epidemic

I test nine hypotheses that are related to the presence of the epidemic:

1. City population size is positively associated with the presence of the homicide epidemic.

2. Population density is positively associated with the presence of the epidemic.

3. Resource deprivation is positively associated with the presence of the epidemic.

4. The unemployment rate is positively associated with the presence of the epidemic.

5. The percent of young people is positively associated with the presence of the epidemic.

6. The proximity to the nearest cocaine hub is positively associated with the presence of an epidemic.

7. The number of cocaine hubs within 500 miles is positively associated with the presence of the epidemic.

8. The averaged homicide rate variable (average homicide rate 1979-1981) is positively associated with the presence of the homicide epidemic.

9. The per capita number of police is negatively associated with the presence of the epidemic.

Hypotheses on the Magnitude of the Epidemic

I test an additional nine hypotheses that are related to the magnitude of the epidemic:

1. City population size is positively associated with the magnitude of the homicide epidemic.

2. Population density is positively associated with the magnitude of the epidemic.

3. Resource deprivation is positively associated with the magnitude of the epidemic.

4. The unemployment rate is positively associated with the magnitude of the epidemic.

5. The percent of young people is positively associated with the magnitude of the epidemic.

6. The proximity to the nearest cocaine hub is positively associated with the magnitude of an epidemic.

7. The number of cocaine hubs within 500 miles is positively associated with the magnitude of the epidemic.

8. The averaged homicide rate variable (average homicide rate 1979-1981) is positively associated with the magnitude of the homicide epidemic.

9. The per capita number of police is negatively associated with the magnitude of the epidemic.

Hypotheses on the Duration of the Epidemic

Finally, I test nine hypotheses that are related to the duration of the epidemic:

1.   City population size is positively associated with the duration of the homicide epidemic.

2.   Population density is positively associated with the duration of the epidemic.

3.   Resource deprivation is positively associated with the duration of the epidemic.

4.   The unemployment rate is positively associated with the duration of the epidemic.

5.   The percent of young people is positively associated with the duration of the epidemic.

6.   The proximity to the nearest cocaine hub is positively associated with the duration of an epidemic.

7.   The number of cocaine hubs within 500 miles is positively associated with the duration of the epidemic.

8.   The averaged homicide rate variable (average homicide rate 1979-1981) is positively associated with the duration of the homicide epidemic.

9.   The per capita number of police is negatively associated with the duration of the epidemic.

Chapter Summary

This chapter provides a review of the criminological literature on the homicide epidemic that occurred in the late 1980s and early 1990s. Most research has focused on Blumstein's (1995) theory linking the influx of crack cocaine to the homicide epidemic. A variety of measures to indicate the timing of the crack influx are used to research the connection between the growth in the crack cocaine market and a subsequent increase in homicide rates. Studies examining this relationship have consistently supported the likelihood of the spread of crack influencing the change in the homicide rate trend.

Research looking at Blumstein's contention that the acquisition of firearms was directly responsible for the increase in homicide rates also provides support for the crack-homicide nexus. Research in this area reveals that gun homicides by youth drove the national homicide increases. Since young minority males are involved to the greatest degree with the crack market, this group is most likely to experience the highest homicide rates.

Blumstein's hypotheses on the geographic diffusion of crack and homicide rates has received less attention than the timing of these two events, but the studies that have been done provide some support for the key hypotheses. The coastal hypothesis, which indicates both the crack market and the homicide rate increases began first in the coastal regions of the U.S. and then spread toward the Midwest, has received some support from geographic analysis based on city-level data. Furthermore, research supports the hypothesis that the largest cities drove the homicide epidemic. Researchers also report that the crack and homicide epidemics first began and ended in the largest cities. This finding supports an epidemic model of hierarchical diffusion that is closely tied with the diffusion of cocaine through the nation.

This chapter also provides a summary of important social variables that are linked to increased homicide rates. Disaggregation of homicide rates reveals that young black males had the highest homicide rates and experienced the greatest magnitude of rate change during the epidemic period. Although theories based on cohort size provide a parsimonious explanation for historical homicide rate changes, this approach fails to account for the unique nature of the homicide trends during the epidemic. During this period homicide rates increased drastically among youth, with a marked increase in lethal violence among categories of young offenders that are historically less inclined toward homicide. The unusual nature of this period requires a perspective that accounts for these changes. Additionally, combining Blumstein's theory with the theoretical extension proposed by Zimring and Hawkins creates a useful theoretical framework to approach the study of the homicide epidemic.

In this chapter I also consider the role of a number of important variables tied to homicide rates. Chief among the predictor variables is resource deprivation. Experts on homicide focus attention on resource deprivation. Other key city-level variables linked to the homicide include population size and density and age structure. I hypothesize that these variables have a positive effect on the presence, magnitude, and duration of the homicide epidemic. On the other hand, theories that focus on the effects of policing indicate that changes in tactics and a high number of police per capita are likely to result in decreased rates of crime, including homicide.

Finally, this chapter presents the formal list of twenty-seven hypotheses that I test in this book. The overarching issues for this book are determining the key variables that affect the presence, magnitude, and duration of the homicide epidemic on the city level. The tests I conduct will help to determine the value of key hypotheses drawn from Blumstein and Zimring and Hawkins. These tests should reveal the importance of city-level variables that may have exacerbated or retarded diffusion of the homicide epidemic.

The next chapter will provide a detailed account of the data that will be used to test the hypotheses proposed in this chapter. Additionally, the next chapter will describe the methods that will be used to determine the length and magnitude of city-level homicide epidemics during the late 1980s and early 1990s as well as the statistical tests that will help to determine the accuracy of the hypotheses.

CHAPTER 4

The Analytical Approach to the Homicide Epidemic: Measuring Variables and Statistical Modeling

The main purpose of this book is to examine the effects of city-level variables on the presence, magnitude, and duration of the homicide epidemic of the late 1980s and early 1990s for major cities in the United States. The key city-level social variables in this analysis include: population size, population density, the percent of the population aged 5-17, the unemployment rate, and resource deprivation. Also included in the analysis are variables based on the proximity of cities to cocaine distribution hubs, the per capita number of police, and a measure of the average homicide rate prior to the onset of the epidemic. The primary assertion of this book is that these variables influenced the characteristics of the homicide epidemic. I presented a series of hypotheses based on the relationships between the independent and dependent variables in chapter 3. This chapter discusses the measures used to calculate the variables that are included in statistical analysis.

Sample Selection

The city is the unit of analysis for this project. Although considerable contemporary criminological research is focused on ever smaller geographic units, such as neighborhoods and census tracts, the city is a useful unit of analysis for research on the national homicide epidemic. Data at this level can provide refined explanations for changes in the national homicide rate trend, and this data is based on information that is readily available.

The national homicide rate is, of course, composed of the aggregate of homicide rates of smaller geographical units, includingcities. The FBI collects crime data from individual police agencies and releases the data annually in the Uniform Crime Report (UCR). Experts focus primarily on city-level homicide rates for tests of theories on the homicide epidemic (e.g., Baumer 1994, Baumer et al. 1998, Cork 1999, Grogger 2000, Grogger and Willis 2000, Johnson, Golub and Dunlap 2000, Ousey and Lee 2002). The goal of this body of research is to understanding how homicide rate changes operate on the city-level and to also to determine to what degree individual city patterns match the national pattern. An analysis at the city-level can not only identify variables that have a significant effect on homicide rate changes, but also identify which cities are affected by these variables to the greatest degree.

City-level research on the homicide epidemic has relied on city sample sizes based on various population size criteria, with the greatest attention focused on large cities. The minimum population cutoffs for inclusion in research have ranged from 100,000 to one million. A common approach is to group large cities into several categories according to size (e.g., under 100,000; 100,000-250,000; 250,000-500,000; 500,000-one million; and over one million). The sample used in this book includes cities in the continental U.S. with populations of 250,000 or more in the year 2001. This cutoff criterion includes all of the largest cities in the U.S. and allows for a reasonably large sample size for statistical analysis. Sixty-eight U.S. cities meet these criteria.

One of the advantages of using UCR homicide data to study attributes of homicide epidemic is that all of the major cities in the United States have longitudinal data covering the time span of the epidemic period[3]. Research focused specifically on the relationship between cocaine measurements and homicide rates within cities is usually limited to those cities for which data on cocaine use or cocaine

---

[3] While the annual UCR data on homicide rates is nearly complete for the sample of cities included in this book, there are some cases in which a city did not report a homicide rate for a given year. I include the results of robustness tests to determine the effect of missing data in the next chapter.

arrests are available. However, I test the relationship between cocaine and the homicide epidemic using measures based on cities' proximity to major cocaine distribution hubs and also the number of cocaine hubs within 500 miles. I calculate these measures for all of the cities in the sample.

Analytical Approach

As noted in chapter 2, the nominal definition of "homicide epidemic" guiding this book is: *A period of time, within a territorial unit, such as a nation or city, in which cases of homicide rise to a level clearly in excess of expectancy and then decline.* The epidemic concept implies a change that involves parameters of both magnitude and duration. I discuss the requirements for the change in magnitude below. Of the cities that I identify as "epidemic" cities, a majority had a homicide rate which rose for series of years. I include one city in the sample that met all requirements for rate changes but only had one year of increase in the fitted regression line. Experts may not agree that this specific case is an example of an epidemic. However, this single city does not greatly influence the outcome of the statistical analyses.

Determining which variables affected how individual cities varied in the presence, magnitude, and duration of the homicide epidemic, requires several steps. The first step in this process is determining if the homicide trend of individual cities is similar to the national trend during the same period. Once I model city rates, I look for the same sorts of trend changes that took place in the national pattern. Although the national rate increase did not begin until 1985, research indicates that individual city trends varied in their timing of both increases and decreases, beginning the period of increase as early as 1981 and ending as late as 1998 (Messner et al. 2005).

Messner et al. (2005) analyzed the size and geographical location of major American cities to test hypotheses drawn from Blumstein's (1995) theory on the homicide epidemic. The approach Messner et al. (2005) used was to fit spline regression functions to the longitudinal homicide rate series for a sample of cities. They used this process to determine regression functions for the expected value of the homicide rates for each city. This statistical method helps to remove the "noise" that masks the "true" homicide rates. I also rely on this method for this study.

I computed homicide rate for each city in the usual way. Homicide counts and total population for the cities included in the sample were recorded from the UCR for the years 1979-2001[4]. I computed annual city-level homicide rates for this period by dividing the number of reported homicides by the annual UCR population figures and multiplying by 100,000.

Applying spline regression techniques to the homicide rate trend of individual cities has a number of important advantages. Spline regression generates a statistical function that smoothes the homicide rate trend. In addition, spline regression can identify points along the trend line where the slope changes significantly. This characteristic is important for studying the epidemic period since the presence of an epidemic in an individual city is marked at the beginning and end by a shift in direction of the trend of expected homicide rate trend. The beginning of an epidemic is noted by a shift from a descending rate to an up tick, marking the start of a series of increasing data points. The end of an epidemic is noted by a shift in the opposite direction, from an increasing series of points to a reversal in trend marked by a downward tick.

Spline regression can identify changes in the trend line, such as a change in the slope of the trend, even with trends in which the number of knots (or breakpoints) is unknown (for a review of spline regression models see Marsh and Cormier 2001). Spline regression also allows for various functional forms, including linear, quadratic, and cubic forms. Techniques of spline regression work even with trends that include segments of unknown functional form. This flexibility is especially useful with data such as the longitudinal homicide trends for individual cities, since an *a priori* prediction of the best-fitting functions for the trend cannot be made. The problem of estimating the number of knots and the shape of each segment between the knots is solved by creating a large number of possible knots and trying several functional forms along the trend line and relying on stepwise regression to determine those knots that are statistically significant and the best functional form of the segments (Marsh 1986; Marsh and Cormier

---

[4] Messner et al. 2005 used this same time frame. 1979 is the first year in UCR data in which precise population values are included for cities.

2001). Contemporary statistical software packages make this process relatively easy.

Spline regression models are statistical models based on dummy variables that are subject to continuity restrictions so that the regression segments between the series of knots always remains connected. Spline regression techniques allow a single equation to express the entire series of data points in a series (Marsh 1986). This attribute is especially useful for longitudinal data that is not linear. A model for an unknown number of knots with unknown functions can be expressed:

$$y = \sum_{j=0}^{3} \beta_{0,j} t^{j} + \sum_{i=1}^{k} \sum_{j=0}^{3} \beta_{i,j} \left(t - t_{i} \right)^{j} D_{i} + \varepsilon$$

In this case, y is the dependent variable, t is time, D is the dummy variable, and ε is the usual error term. The dummy variable is equal to zero until the point in the trend line where t is greater than t_{i} (where $i = 1,...,k$), when the dummy variables are equal to one. k knots are indicated by t_{i}. Stepwise regression selects the location of the knots at an imposed level of statistical significance as well as the functional form (linear, quadratic, or cubic) of each of the segments between the knots. I follow the example of Messner et al. (2005) and use a significance level of .05. Both the number of knots and the form of the function fit for any given trend line may vary depending on the level of significance imposed.

A city experienced an epidemic only if in the fitted trend line it experienced an upturn in rate after a declining rate and the upward trend was also be followed by a downturn. Both the upturn and the downturn must take place sometime within the specified period (1980-2000) to be included. This requirement is imposed to insure that the epidemic period for individual cities falls at or near the national epidemic period, which began in the late 1980s and peaked in the early 1990s.

Some care must be taken with statistical tests that look at the effect of independent variables on magnitude and duration. Although only cities that experienced an epidemic have obvious values for magnitude and duration, I will follow Messner et al.'s strategy of adopting Tobit regression techniques to include information on the entire sample of the cities to estimate regression lines. Tobit analysis is used for a regression model that creates a latent variable to account for observations that are truncated (or censored) (Tobin 1958). The parameters of the latent variable are estimated by maximum likelihood.

One of the advantages of Tobit analysis is that it is generalizable to data that are censored on the left or the right. In the case of the epidemic parameters the data are right censored since all of the cities had the possibility of experiencing an epidemic during the time period under investigation. The cities that did not experience the epidemic have censored data.

The stochastic model underlying Tobin's model can be expressed with the following model:

$$y_i = X_i\beta + u_i \quad \text{if } X_i\beta + u_i > 0$$
$$= 0 \quad\quad\quad \text{if } X_i\beta + u_i \leq 0, \ \ i = 1, 2, \ldots, N$$

where N is the number of observations, y is the dependent variable, X is a vector of independent variables, β is a vector of unknown coefficients, and u is an independently distributed error term assumed to be normal with zero mean and constant variance.

Tobin's model assumes an underlying, stochastic index equal to $\left(X_i\beta + u_i\right)$ which is observed only when it is positive (i.e., above the limiting value). The expected value of y in the model is:

$$Ey = X\beta F(z) + \sigma f(z)$$

where $z = X\beta / \sigma$, $f(z)$ is the unit normal density, and $F(z)$ is the cumulative normal distribution function. In addition, McDonald and Moffitt (1980) show that the expected value of y for observations above the limit, e.g., y^*, is $X\beta$ plus the expected value of the truncated normal error term:

$$Ey^* = E(y \mid y > 0)$$
$$= E(y \mid u > -X\beta)$$
$$= X\beta + \sigma f(z)/F(z).$$

The Tobit model contains three pieces of information: the expected value of all observations, Ey, the expected value conditional upon being above the limit, Ey^*, and the probability of being above the limit, $F(z)$.

Tobit techniques allow testing on samples that includes information on every case in the sample, even if the sample has cases with missing values. This approach overcomes the bias that is involved with the alternative method of simple ignoring cases that do not have values above some cut-off criteria.

I conduct tests on city-level variation in presence of the epidemic with logistic regression (for an overview of logistic regression see DeMaris 1995). Logistic regression allows for tests involving binary response variables. For example, for this study, a city either experienced an epidemic or it did not. The presence of the epidemic is therefore binary.

If χ is a vector of explanatory variables and $P = \Pr(Y = 1 \mid \chi)$ is the response probability modeled, then the linear logistic model has the form:

$$\text{logit}(P) \equiv \log(\frac{P}{1-P}) = \alpha + \beta' \chi$$

Where α is the intercept parameter and β is the vector of slope parameters.

The logistic technique fits linear logistic regression models and odds ratio estimates are computed with the standard parameter output. The logit transformation on the probability of P is $\log(\frac{P}{1-P})$ where log refers to the natural logarithm and the term $\frac{P}{1-P}$ is the odds, which is a ratio of probabilities. The log odds can be modeled as a linear function of the predictor set, which is based on this logistic regression model:

$$\log(\frac{P}{1-P}) = \alpha + \beta_1 \chi_1 + \beta_2 \chi_2 + ... + \beta_k \chi_k$$

In this study, I model the probability of experiencing the homicide epidemic divided by the probability of not experiencing the epidemic.

Dependent Variables

The dependent variables I use in this analysis are derived from the city-level spline regression functions for the expected homicide rate. I derive three key characteristics of the homicide epidemic from plots created by spline regression functions: presence, magnitude, and duration.

Presence

The presence variable simply refers to whether or not a city experienced a period of homicide rate increase that was both proceeded by and followed by a declining homicide rate. Thirty-three out of the sixty-eight cities in the sample did not experience an epidemic according to these criteria. As Messner et al. (2005) point out, cities that did not experience the epidemic follow four general patterns. The patterns can be seen in the following four example cities, shown with a line indicating actual homicide rate from 1979-2001 and another line showing the regression line fitted by the spline regression technique. The fitted spline regression line in each graph is the line that generally falls within the more volatile pattern representing the actual homicide rates.

The first two examples, San Jose and Denver show cities with downward trends throughout the period of interest. San Jose's rate declines at a constant rate, while Denver's rate declines at a slow rate followed by a more precipitous decline:

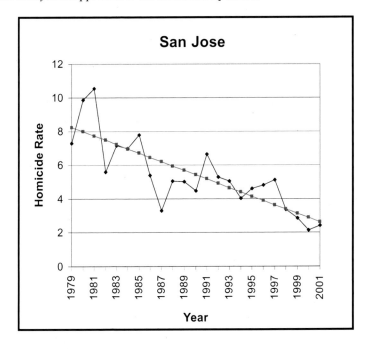

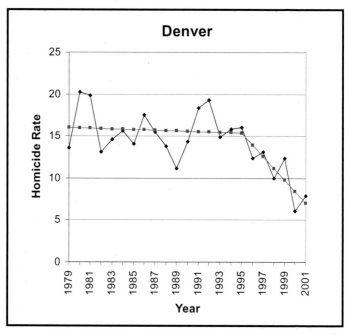

The second two examples show the other types of patterns found
for the fitted spline regression.   Indianapolis shows a pattern of steady
incline over the period, while the pattern for Virginia Beach is a steady
incline followed by a more precipitous decline:

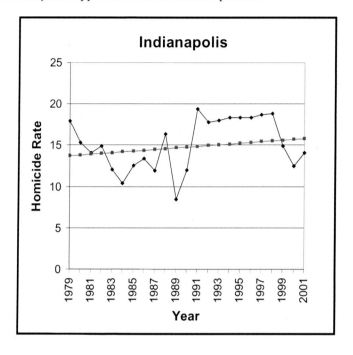

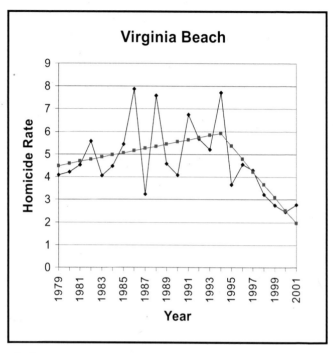

Magnitude

The magnitude variable refers to the size of the increase in homicide rates during the epidemic period. I determine the magnitude by subtracting the initial value of the expected homicide rate from the highest value (the peak rate) of the expected homicide rate during the epidemic period. This measure represents the absolute difference in homicide rate increases. An alternative measure of magnitude is the percent change. I run tests including each of these measures to determine how the independent variables affect each magnitude measure. Of course, only cities in the sample that experienced an epidemic cycle have an obvious measure for this variable. However, the Tobit regression techniques still allow for the inclusion of information for cities that did not experience the epidemic.

The magnitude of the epidemic varied widely for cities in this sample. For example, comparing the magnitude of two cities demonstrates the variation:

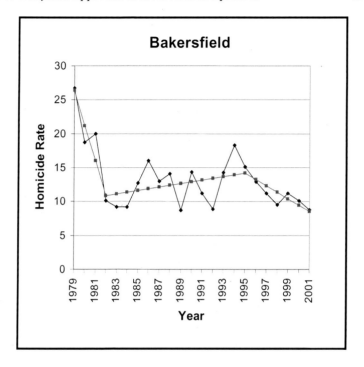

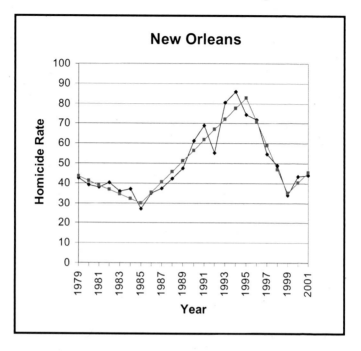

For the two examples shown above, the range of the magnitude of the homicide epidemic clearly varied widely. While the rate for Bakersfield stayed within the boundaries of 10 to 15 for the entire period of the epidemic, the rate for New Orleans grew dramatically from a rate around 30 to a height at the peak of the epidemic above 80. The range of the magnitude for homicide rates during the epidemic was about 10 times greater for New Orleans compared to Bakersfield.

Duration

The duration variable refers to the length of time that a homicide epidemic lasts. I determined the duration by summing the number of years from the initial point that the expected homicide rate begins to incline until the series reaches the highest value before declining. Comparing two cities in the sample demonstrates the level of variability in the sample:

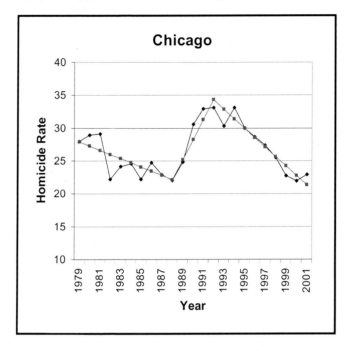

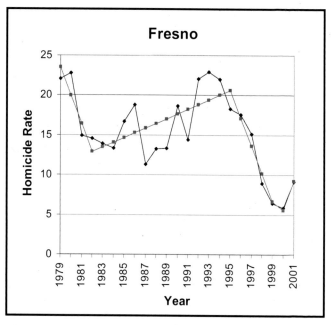

The two cities above provide some idea of the variability for the
duration of the epidemic period.   Chicago experienced a relatively
short epidemic period, lasting only 5 years. Fresno, on the other hand,
experienced a much longer epidemic period, lasting 14 years, nearly
three times longer than Chicago's epidemic.

Cities that had inclines or declines of the fitted rate outside of the
time period under investigation are not considered "epidemic" cities
(i.e., cities that did not have both an incline and a decline between 1980
and 2000). Two main reasons explain why. First, to argue that a series
of inclines that last over two decades can be considered an epidemic is
difficult, especially following the definition of "epidemic" used in this
study. Second, if a city did not experience an incline and decline in the
period under investigation, to argue that the rate changes are tied to the
national epidemic is difficult, considering the national epidemic took
place in the late 1980s and early 1990s.

Independent Variables

Population Size and Density

City population size and density are positively related to crime in general and are also highlighted as important variables in regard to the homicide epidemic (e.g., Blumstein 1995, Messner et al. 2005). The variable city size is a measure of the total population count and population density is a measure of the number of people per square mile. I took the population count for cities from annual UCR data for each city. The County and City Data Book provide the data for the population density variable (U.S. Department of Commerce 1983 and 1994). Since the distributions of population size and density are right skewed, the measures I use in the statistical tests are normalized by transforming them using the natural logarithms of the original values.

I predict that city population size and density had positive effects on all three of the dependent variables. Blumstein (1995) emphasizes the nature of the crack cocaine market, which involves large numbers of buyers, sellers, and transactions, as well as the presence of firearms. Large cities have more potential buyers, sellers, and, therefore, also a potential for more transactions. The number of deadly disputes increases with the number of transactions.

Meta-analysis of homicide research reveals that population density is a consistent positive covariate with homicide rates (Land et al. 1990). Densely populated areas could be more susceptible to an increase in homicide rates related to the crack cocaine markets because more drug sales in a given area increase the likelihood of lethal dispute resolutions. Consider, for example, the increased likelihood of territorial disputes when armed drug dealers are in close proximity to each other or the increased likelihood of armed robbery of drug dealers with a higher density of potential assailants. I predict that smaller, less densely populated cities are less likely to have experienced a homicide epidemic, and for such cities that did experience an epidemic, the magnitude and duration are not as great compared to larger, more densely populated cities.

Percent Young

The County and City Data Book provide the data for the percent young variable (U.S. Department of Commerce 1983 and 1994). I computed this variable by taking the number of people aged 5-17 and dividing by the total city population. I include this variable to test the effects of a large proportion of youth on the epidemic parameters. Tests including the presence variable the values are from 1980, while tests with the magnitude and duration variables include the values from 1990.

Unemployment Rate

The unemployment rate variable is also based on data from the County and City Data Book (U.S. Department of Commerce 1983 and 1994). The unemployment rate is based on the percent of the total civilian labor force. Although research on this variable fails to find a consistent relationship with homicide rates, one suspicion is that high unemployment rates might lead more people to join in black market activities like crack sales. Tests including the presence variable use unemployment values from 1980, while tests including the magnitude and duration variables use the values from 1990.

Resource Deprivation

A principal components index yields the resource deprivation variable. Using the principle components index for resource deprivation follows conventional practices (e.g., Land et al. 1990, Messner et al. 2005, Ousey and Lee 2002). The variables included in this index are: the percent of families below the poverty line, median family income, percent of female headed households with no husband present, and percent black of the population. The data for these variables are from the County and City Data Book (U.S. Department of Commerce 1983 and 1994).

The eigenvectors for the principal components analysis in for the 1980 values, for example, are:

Percent Black	0.475970
Median Family Income	-.473535
Poverty Rate	0.524325
Percent of Female Headed Households	0.523737

Since detailed census data is not available on an annual basis for cities, I use measures taken from different times depending on the dependent variable in the test. For the presence variable the median family income measure and the percent of families below the poverty level are 1979 values, while the percent of female-headed households variable and percent black are 1980 values. The use of these years serves to provide a baseline of variable measures for these city-level characteristics before the national homicide epidemic began.

For tests including the magnitude and duration variables, I use values taken from the next available set of city-level data from the 1994 County and City Data Book. In this case the median family income measure, the percent of families below the poverty level and the percent of female-headed households variables are from 1989, and the percent black variable is from 1990.

Average Homicide Rate

The statistical analysis also includes a measure of the average homicide rate 1979-1981. I derived this data from the UCR. I calculated this measure by summing the homicide rates for each year and then dividing by three. I include this variable to determine if preexisting homicide rates had any effect on the parameters of the epidemic.

Proximity

Blumstein (1995) makes a number of assertions about the relationship between the location of major cities in the U.S. and the diffusion of the homicide epidemic. While research considers Blumstein's coastal hypothesis (the prediction that the epidemic was primarily focused on the coasts of the U.S.) (e.g., Cork 1999, Messner 2003), no research considers the relationship between major cocaine hubs (cities identified by law enforcement agencies as the principal distribution points for cocaine) and the presence, magnitude, and duration of the epidemic.

Variations in cost and levels of purity of cocaine relative to the distance from source cities highlights the importance of the location of cocaine distribution hubs. The National Drug Intelligence Center (NDIC) (2001) reports the following:

> Purity levels from 80 to 90 percent are common throughout the New England, New York/New Jersey, Mid-Atlantic, Great Lakes, Southeast, Florida/Caribbean, Southwest, and Pacific Regions. In the West Central Region, cocaine purity varies widely. In urban areas throughout the region, purity levels are comparable to those in the major market areas of the East. In suburban and rural areas, purity can be as low as 20 percent. Wholesale and retail cocaine prices reflect the same general

trend: prices for high purity cocaine are lowest in major markets and higher in areas farther away. Wholesale prices generally range from $16,000 to $22,000 per kilogram but have been reported as low as $9,000 in Houston and as high as $35,000 in St. Louis. Retail prices range from $75 to $100 per gram but have been reported as low as $20 per gram in Miami and as high as $125 in Denver (retrieved online at http://www.usdoj.gov/ndic/pubs/647/cocaine.htm#Foot4).

If cost and availability influence consumption of cocaine (following the laws of supply and demand), then cities in which cocaine is more expensive and in lesser quantities should have fewer consumers. If crack cocaine dealing and using is positively related to the homicide epidemic, then the distance between the major distribution points and large cities should be negatively related to the presence, magnitude, and duration of the epidemic.

The NDIC identifies major cocaine distribution cities based on information from federal and local law enforcement agencies, which base their information on arrests and drug seizures. I calculated the distance between the sample cities and cocaine hubs using Mapquest, a software program based on driving distance between cities. To insure the validity of the distances, I checked the measures Mapquest generated against surface distances between cities based on longitude and latitude with software from the U.S. Department of Agriculture.

Driving distance between cities is a good measure of the distance cocaine is transported based on information from the NDIC that cocaine is frequently confiscated by law enforcement agencies from private vehicles and tractor-trailer trucks. I will also include models using a measure of the number of cocaine hubs within 500 miles to account for the presence of multiple distribution locations that could serve a city. Since no research has considered the relationship between proximity to cocaine distribution hubs and the presence, magnitude, and duration of the homicide epidemic, this largely exploratory research could be extended if the study uncovers significant relationships.

I predict that the proximity variable will positively affect all three dependent variables. The closer a city is in proximity to cocaine hubs, the more likely it will be to have an epidemic. For cities that experienced an epidemic the closer the proximity to cocaine hubs, the more likely the epidemic will be of greater magnitude and duration.

Number of Police Officers

I calculated the per capita number of police officers variable from the UCR city-level data on the number of police officers divided by the total city population and then multiplied by 100,000. Tests on the presence of the epidemic that compare cities that did not experience the epidemic to cities that did will use per capita police values from 1980 for cities that did not experience the epidemic and values from the first year of the epidemic for cities that did experience the epidemic. Likewise, tests on magnitude and duration will use values from 1990 for cities that did not experience the epidemic and values from the last year of the epidemic for cities that experienced the epidemic.

Summary

The purpose of this book is to test the effects of city-level variables on the presence, magnitude, and duration of the homicide epidemic. The independent variables I use in the tests include city population size and density, the percent of the population aged 5-17, the unemployment rate, a resource deprivation index, an average homicide rate, a measure of the proximity to the nearest cocaine distribution hub, the number of hubs within 500 miles, and change in the per capita number of police officers. I derived the dependent variables from the application of spline regression techniques, which removes the "noise" in the trend line for city-level homicide rates, revealing the systematic effects of the trend. The application of spline regression reveals the presence, magnitude, and duration of the epidemic.

One of the unique contributions of this book is the inclusion of the effects of the proximity to the nearest major cocaine hub and the number of hubs within 500 miles on the spatial diffusion of homicide rates. While Blumstein (1995) proposes a number of hypotheses based on geography, he does not specifically address the issue of the transportation routes of cocaine. Tests on the proximity variables should help reveal the role of these variables on the parameters of the homicide epidemic.

I also examine the effects of city population size, population density, the percent of the population aged 5-17, the unemployment rate, and resource deprivation on the presence, magnitude, and duration of the epidemic. Finally, I test the effects of a policing measure. This measure is the per capita number of police, which has been linked to the decline in homicide rates (Levitt 2004). The next chapter presents the descriptive statistics and results of statistical analysis.

CHAPTER 5

The Social Context of Major Cities and Tests on the Epidemic Parameters

This chapter tests the hypotheses presented in chapter 3. The chapter begins by reviewing the robustness tests conducted to determine the effects of missing data points on the computation of the dependent variables. Next, I discuss the characteristics of the independent variables included in the statistical analysis. I go on to discuss the characteristics of the three dependent variables of the homicide epidemic: presence, magnitude, and duration.

I then present the results of correlations between the variables and the results of regression analysis testing the hypotheses proposed in chapter 3. The regression analysis includes multivariate logistic regressions focused on the presence of the epidemic and multivariate Tobit regressions focused on the change in absolute magnitude of the change in homicide rates, the percent change in the homicide rates, and the duration of the homicide epidemic. Finally, I provide a brief conclusion summarizing the chapter.

Robustness Tests

I selected the dependent variables included in this study based on the application of spline regression techniques applied to homicide rates. I calculated the homicide rates for each city from UCR homicide and population counts. I performed robustness tests for the years in which cities have missing data to determine what effect missing points may have on the conclusions about the best-fitting spline regression. Generally, the homicide count data from the UCR is complete. The sample of 68 cities that I used for the statistical tests included 19 cities with 1 missing year of data, 1 city with 2 missing years, and only 1 city with 3 missing years.

Robustness tests are useful in ascertaining the effect that missing data may have on the structural form taken by the spline regression which is used in this case to indicate the fitted homicide rate during the period under investigation (1979-2001). That robustness tests are conducted in this case is especially important, since shifting the form or number of segments in the fitted homicide rate could affect the values of each of the dependent variables, and thereby alter the outcome of the statistical tests.

I applied the spline regression techniques two different ways for cities that had missing data on homicide counts for a particular year. First, I applied the regression on the series of data that were available and did not include a value for any missing data point. Second, I interpolated a value for the missing year in the usual way, by summing the homicide rate from the year before and year after the missing year and dividing the sum by two to compute a mean score for homicide rate. I then inserted the mean score into the data matrix and applied the spline regression techniques based on the original homicide rate values and the interpolated value.

The results of the robustness tests on the city of Miami illustrate the procedure. Figure 5.1 shows the plotted graph for Miami in which the homicide rate for the year 1988 is missing. Figure 5.2 shows the expected homicide rate I computed with the spline regression techniques on the series of data presented in figure 5.1, without a homicide rate value for 1988. Next, I calculated and inserted an average value for 1988. Figure 5.3 shows the expected homicide rate that I computed with the spline regression techniques on the series of data presented in figure 5.1, except that in this case, a mean homicide rate value of 33.94 was computed for 1988 based on the homicide rate values from the year before the missing point (1987, which had a rate of 33.24) and the year after the missing point (1989, which had a rate of 34.63).

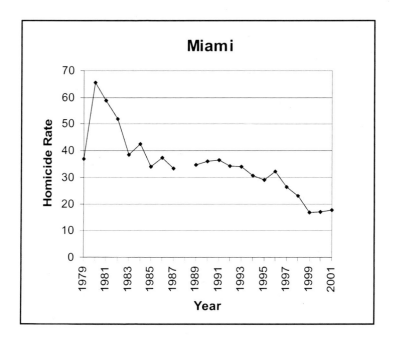

Figure 5.1. Homicide Rate for Miami from UCR with 1988 Missing.

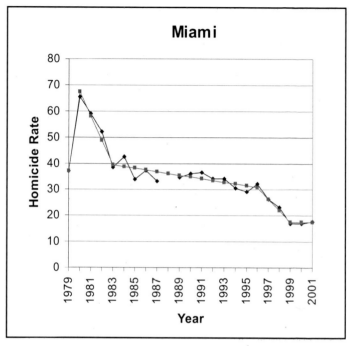

Figure 5.2. Homicide Rate Miami with 1988 Missing and Fitted Rate.

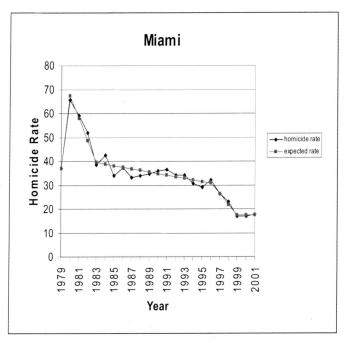

Figure 5.3. Homicide Rate for the City of Miami with Interpolated Value for 1988 and Fitted Rate.

Visual inspection of the above figures reveals little reason to suspect that in this case the missing data point significantly influences the computation of the dependent variables. Whether the missing data point is simply not included in the observed homicide rate series or whether a value is interpolated based on the values on either side of the missing value, the spline regression line remains unchanged. To confirm this result is the case for every city with missing values, I calculated the values for the three dependent variables using both the fitted series without the missing data points and with the interpolated values inserted for missing data points for each city.

Table 5.1 presents the values for the dependent variables for cities with missing data values using the two approaches. The values on the left panel are the result of the application of spline regression to the homicide rate series with missing data without the insertion of interpolated values. The values on the right side are the result of the application of spline regression to the homicide rate series with interpolated values inserted in place of missing data.

Table 5.1. Results of Robustness Test for Cities with Missing Data

Cities	Series with Missing Data			Series with Interpolated Values		
	A	B	C	A	B	C
Albuquerque	4.56	50.22	14	4.56	50.22	14
Baltimore	22.32	85.95	10	21.74	83.87	10
Buffalo	18.65	178.47	7	*	*	*
Cincinnati	*	*	*	*	*	*
Colorado Springs	*	*	*	*	*	*
Houston	*	*	*	*	*	*
Indianapolis	19.15	8.12	14	*	*	*
Jacksonville	*	*	*	*	*	*
Las Vegas	6.77	55.40	11	6.77	55.40	11
Lexington	*	*	*	*	*	*
Louisville	10.26	78.80	10	8.95	68.01	11
Miami	*	*	*	*	*	*
Minneapolis	16.35	258.70	13	15.03	225.34	13
Oakland	13.46	45.43	9	13.92	45.52	8
Omaha	*	*	*	*	*	*
Philadelphia	15.1	102.17	6	15.1	102.17	6
San Francisco	4.99	41.97	6	4.99	41.97	6
Tampa	*	*	*	*	*	*
Toledo	5.5	71.52	9	4.9	62.58	9
Tucson	*	*	*	*	*	*
St Petersburg	8.7	112.26	6	8.7	112.26	6

*No Epidemic Present
A = Absolute Magnitude Change
B = Percent Change
C = Duration

Two cases, Buffalo and Indianapolis, stand out. These two cities are epidemic cities when the spline regression is based on the series with missing data. However, they are non-epidemic cities when interpolated values are inserted in place of the missing data points. The inclusion of interpolated values either has no effect or only a slight effect on the dependent variables for the other 19 cities with missing data points. Additionally, a majority of the cities with missing data maintain their status as epidemic or non-epidemic cities regardless of the inclusion or exclusion of the interpolated values.

The comparison of dependent variable values with and without interpolated values demonstrates the sensitivity of the spline regression techniques to missing data points. Notice that one of the two cities with the greatest disparity of dependent variable values is Indianapolis, which has three missing data points in a row, the greatest number of missing data points in the sample. Not interpolating values for this city would present a highly inaccurate data series.

I include interpolated values for cities with missing data to determine the values for the dependent variables for inclusion in the statistical tests I discuss below. This decision is based in part on the results of the comparison of dependent variable values with and without interpolated values, which demonstrates that in a majority of cases this correction does not significantly alter the dependent variable values. However, the best-fitting multivariate statistical model does change for one of the dependent variables if the spline regression techniques are applied to the city homicide series without inserting interpolated values. I will address this point in the discussion of multivariate model selection below.

I based the decision to use interpolated values on the preference for homicide rate data series that are as close to accurate as possible. Although the interpolated values may not precisely reflect the actual homicide rate for missing years, the interpolated values create a data series that more closely mirrors a probable homicide rate data series than a series in which no values are reported for a year or more.

Independent Variables

One of the benefits of looking at city-level data, in which the cities are not aggregated into groups based on population size, is that this approach provides a good idea of the distribution of variables in individual cities and allows for comparison between cities. These points are especially valid for the purposes of this book, which in part, involves geographically based measurements. A key contribution of the review of variables in this chapter is that I identify cities with the lowest and highest measurements. The identification of these cities provides an idea of the distribution of these variables across space and time. This step also reveals any patterns in the distribution of the highest and lowest values of the variables. Finally, this step identifies if the maximum and minimum values of the variables are extreme outliers or if the cities between these poles are similar in their scores.

I address a number of important questions by looking at the levels of the independent variables and the changes in levels over the epidemic period. For example: do the same cities have high or low scores across the various independent variables? Do the patterns of distribution change or remain static between 1980 and 1990? Do regional patterns emerge that might provide a clue as to the geographic characteristics of the epidemic?

I have identified a series of key city-level variables that research links to homicide rates in general. Research links the following city-level variables to homicide rates: the population size, the population density, the percent of the population aged 5 to 17, the unemployment rate, and an index of resource deprivation that consists of the percent of the population that is black, the percent of female-headed households, the median income, and the percent of families below the poverty line. I also include the 1979-1981 average homicide rate for each city. Table 5.2 presents a summary of the descriptive statistics for each of these variables (aside from population size which I present in greater detail in table 5.3 and discuss below).

Table 5.2. Descriptive Statistics for Independent Variables

Variables	Mean	Std Dev	Min	Max
Population Density 1980	4,887.41	4,093.1	668	23,455
Population Density 1990	4,900.59	3,994.75	746	23,671
Percent Young 1980	19.05	3.06	12.5	25.9
Percent Young 1990	17.24	2.39	10.8	23.2
Unemployment 1980	9.49	3.02	4.7	20.3
Unemployment 1991	6.8	2.09	3.2	13.1
Percent Black 1980	21.67	17.3	1.21	70.24
Percent Black 1990	23.14	18.05	1.85	75.67
Female Headed Households 1980	13.8	5.1	7.38	28.31
Female Headed Households 1990	14.95	4.69	8.64	30.36
Median Income 1979	18,862.66	2,653.17	11,989	25,598
Median Income 1989	27,044.43	5,364.13	16,925	46,206
Percent Families Below Poverty 1979	12.07	4.89	3.8	29.9
Percent Families Below Poverty 1989	14.09	5.58	4.3	29
Averaged Homicide Rate 1979-1981	19.47	12.12	3.02	53.78

Table 5.2 provides two measures for each of the independent variables. The County and City Data Book from1983 provides the first set of measures, and I use these measures in the tests of the presence of the epidemic (U. S. Department of Commerce).

The County and City Data Book from 1994 provides the second set of measures, and I use these measures in tests of the duration and magnitude of the epidemic (see the discussion in chapter 4 on data selection)[5] (U. S. Department of Commerce). This table presents the values of the key variables from circa 1980 and circa 1990[6].

Each time period captures a snapshot of the city-level context for these variables. The reason I use these two years is that they predict characteristics of the epidemic that took place at different times. I use the first set of measurements (from circa 1980) to indicate the context of the cities before the homicide epidemic began. Since the cities in the sample began the epidemic between 1980 and 1990, this snapshot provides a picture of the context at the onset of the epidemic. I use the second set of measurements (from circa 1990) to indicate the context of the cities during the epidemic and before they reached the maximum magnitude and the end of the epidemic (marked by a downturn in expected homicide rates).

I contrast the city sample values with the national values for variables where this contrast provides an idea of how well the sample represents the nation. Finally, I make note of any regional patterns or cases in which cities maintain the highest or lowest scores between the values from around 1980 and 1990.

---

[5] The one exception for the date of the independent variable values is St. Petersburg, which is the only city in the sample that experienced an epidemic decline prior to 1990. For this city, the values taken from the 1983 County and City Data Book will be used in place of values from circa 1990.

[6] The income measures (including median income and percent of families below poverty) are from 1979 and 1989. The unemployment rate is from 1982 and 1991. All other variables are from 1980 and 1990.

Table 5.3. Sample Cities, Populations for 2001 and 1980, Year of Homicide Upturn and Year of Homicide Downturn

State	City	Pop. 2001	Pop. 1980	Yr of Upturn	Yr of Downturn
AL	Mobile	255,551	199,411	1984	1997
AZ	Mesa	410,026	269,993	*	*
AZ	Phoenix	1,366,542	772,884	*	*
AZ	Tucson	503,461	331,506	*	*
CA	Anaheim	334,110	218,468	1982	1993
CA	Bakersfield	251,648	112,282	1982	1995
CA	Fresno	435,600	215,396	1982	1995
CA	Long Beach	470,099	356,906	1986	1993
CA	Los Angeles	3,763,486	2,952,511	1986	1993
CA	Oakland	406,908	338,721	1985	1993
CA	Riverside	259,908	169,895	1982	1994
CA	Sacramento	414,582	274,547	*	*
CA	San Diego	1,246,136	874,826	1984	1991
CA	San Francisco	763,146[7]	674,150	1987	1993
CA	San Jose	913,513	628,106	*	*
CA	Santa Ana	344,258	205,730	*	*
CO	Aurora	283,876	158,249	*	*
CO	Colorado Springs	370,661	206,979	*	*
CO	Denver	569,653	489,318	*	*
D.C.	D.C	571,822	635,233	1985	1990
FL	Jacksonville	754,679	542,795	*	*
FL	Miami	371,863	335,718	*	*
FL	St. Petersburg	254,664	233,532	1983	1989
FL	Tampa	311,310	268,709	*	*

[7] Population for San Francisco is from 2000.

Table 5.3. Sample Cities, Populations for 2001 and 1980, Year of Homicide Upturn and Year of Homicide Downturn (continued)

State	City	Pop. 2001	Pop. 1980	Yr of Upturn	Yr of Downturn
GA	Atlanta	426,511	422,474	1983	1990
IL	Chicago	2,910,709	2,986,419	1988	1992
IN	Indianapolis	798,251	698,753	*	*
KS	Wichita	345,081	279,352	*	*
KY	Lexington	262,045	203,082	*	*
KY	Louisville	257,739	298,313	1986	1997
LA	New Orleans	484,289	557,761	1985	1995
MD	Baltimore	660,826	784,554	1983	1993
MA	Boston	591,944	562,582	1989	1990
MI	Detroit	956,283	1,197,325	*	*
MN	Minneapolis	386,726	370,163	1983	1996
MN	St. Paul	290,234	268,443	1982	1996
MO	Kansas City	444,267	446,865	1984	1992
MO	St. Louis	350,336	450,790	1986	1993
NB	Omaha	390,456	312,919	*	*
NV	Las Vegas	1,117,763	385,396	1985	1996
NJ	Newark	275,823	330,104	*	*
NM	Albuquerque	451,098	328,827	1982	1996
NY	Buffalo	293,187	357,384	*	*
NY	NYC	8,023,018	7,035,348	1985	1991
NC	Charlotte	636,459	310,794	1986	1992
NC	Raleigh	280,791	148,429	*	*
OH	Cincinnati	331,880	383,114	*	*
OH	Cleveland	479,263	572,657	1986	1992
OH	Columbus	712,748	562,416	1985	1992
OH	Toledo	314,183	354,558	1985	1994
GA	Atlanta	426,511	422,474	1983	1990
IL	Chicago	2,910,709	2,986,419	1988	1992

**Table 5.3. Sample Cities, Populations for 2001 and 1980,
Year of Homicide Upturn and Year of Homicide
Downturn (continued)**

State	City	Pop. 2001	Pop. 1980	Yr of Upturn	Yr of Downturn
IN	Indianapolis	798,251	698,753	*	*
KS	Wichita	345,081	279,352	*	*
KY	Lexington	262,045	203,082	*	*
KY	Louisville	257,739	298,313	1986	1997
LA	New Orleans	484,289	557,761	1985	1995
MD	Baltimore	660,826	784,554	1983	1993
MA	Boston	591,944	562,582	1989	1990
MI	Detroit	956,283	1,197,325	*	*
MN	Minneapolis	386,726	370,163	1983	1996
MN	St. Paul	290,234	268,443	1982	1996
MO	Kansas City	444,267	446,865	1984	1992
MO	St. Louis	350,336	450,790	1986	1993
NB	Omaha	390,456	312,919	*	*
NV	Las Vegas	1,117,763	385,396	1985	1996
NJ	Newark	275,823	330,104	*	*
NM	Albuquerque	451,098	328,827	1982	1996
NY	Buffalo	293,187	357,384	*	*
NY	New York City	8,023,018	7,035,348	1985	1991
NC	Charlotte	636,459	310,794	1986	1992
NC	Raleigh	280,791	148,429	*	*
OH	Cincinnati	331,880	383,114	*	*
OH	Cleveland	479,263	572,657	1986	1992
OH	Columbus	712,748	562,416	1985	1992
OH	Toledo	314,183	354,558	1985	1994

Table 5.3. Sample Cities, Populations for 2001 and 1980, Year of Homicide Upturn and Year of Homicide Downturn (continued)

State	City	Pop. 2001	Pop. 1980	Yr of Upturn	Yr of Downturn
OK	Oklahoma City	507,517	401,577	*	*
OK	Tulsa	394,125	355,766	*	*
OR	Portland	537,081	364,419	*	*
PA	Philadelphia	1,518,302	1,681,175	1984	1990
PA	Pittsburgh	341,414	424,205	1989	1994
TN	Memphis	655,898	644,957	*	*
TN	Nashville	555,059	452,025	*	*
TX	Arlington	340,525	161,192	*	*
TX	Austin	671,462	343,425	*	*
TX	Corpus Christi	283,750	230,715	*	*
TX	Dallas	1,215,553	900,104	1983	1991
TX	El Paso	576,453	425,122	1987	1993
TX	Fort Worth	546,828	382,679	*	*
TX	Houston	1,997,965	1,619,644	*	*
TX	San Antonio	1,170,622	788,049	1988	1993
VA	Virginia Beach	431,819	260,680	*	*
WA	Seattle	572,345	491,897	*	*
WI	Milwaukee	601,229	633,845	1984	1991

Population Size

Table 5.3 shows the 68 cities in the sample, along with city populations in 1980 and in 2001, and the year of incline and decline for cities that experienced a homicide epidemic. These are the most populous cities in the continental United States in 2001, all with populations above 250,000. The cities range in population from 8,023,018 for New York City[8] in 2001 to 251,648 for Bakersfield in 2001. The four largest cities in the sample for 2001 include New York City, Los Angeles with 3,763,486 residents, Chicago with 2,910,709 residents, and Houston with 1,997,965 residents. Ten cities in the sample had a population greater than one million in 2001. The cities with the fewest residents in the sample for 2001 include Bakersfield with 251,648 residents, St. Petersburg with 254,664 residents, Mobile with 255,551 residents, and Louisville with 257,739 residents. A total of 12 cities in the sample had 2001 populations below 300,000 residents.

In 1980 the most populous cities were New York City with 7,035,348 residents, Chicago with 2,986,419 residents, Los Angeles with 2,952,511 residents, and Philadelphia with 1,681,175 residents. The cities with the smallest populations in the sample in 1980 include Bakersfield with 112,282 residents, Raleigh with 148,429 residents, Aurora with 158,249 residents, and Arlington with 161,192 residents.

Generally the same cities with the largest populations in 1980 remain the largest in 2001. On the other hand, only one city is on the list of the four cities with the fewest residents in the sample in both 1980 and 2001. The population change for cities in the decades that encompass the homicide epidemic is an important consideration since the fluctuation of population size may have implications for the change in homicide rates.

Population Density

Population density is a significant variable associated with the homicide epidemic (Messner et al. 2005). Messner et al. (2005) report that densely populated cities were in the vanguard for rising and falling homicide rates. Table 5.2 reveals very little change in distribution of the descriptive statistics for population density between 1980 and 1990 measures: the mean, standard deviation, and even the minimum and

---

[8] Cities will all be identified only by their city name in this chapter. A complete list of cities and their corresponding states is presented in table 5.3.

maximum values indicate a highly similar pattern. A careful look at the cities in the sample also indicates that the same cities that had the least dense populations in 1980, including Oklahoma City with 668 people per square mile, Jacksonville with 712 people per square mile, and Lexington with 117 people per square mile, also had the least dense populations in 1990, with values of 746 people per square mile, 871 people per square mile, and 817 people per square mile respectively.

The same symmetry can be seen in the cities with the greatest density as well. The cities with the highest density in 1980 were New York City with 23,455 people per square mile, San Francisco with 14,633 people per square mile, and Newark with 13,622 people per square mile. New York City and San Francisco remained the most densely populated cities in 1990 with values of 23,671 people per square mile and 15,609 people per square mile, respectively. Although Newark slipped from third to sixth most densely populated with a value of 11,254, the same cities make up the top six most densely populated in both 1980 and 1990. The general stability of the population density variable is notable, especially considering that prior research finds that density is an important variable for the timing of the epidemic at the city level (Messner et al. 2005). More densely populated cities may be more susceptible to a homicide epidemic.

Percent Young

The next variable presented in table 5.2 is the percent of the population aged five through seventeen years old, which is labeled "Percent Young". The proportion of young people is important reflecting both the notion that, in general, young people have the highest rates of violent criminality and more specifically for this study, the finding that young populations were at high risk for homicide offense and victimization (see e.g., Cook and Laub 1998). The relative size of the youth population within sample cities reflects national demographic shifts. The mean value for this variable is slightly greater in 1980 when the rate was 19.05 percent, than in 1990 when the rate was 17.24 percent.

Cities with the smallest percent of population between the ages of 5 to 17 in 1980 were found mainly on the West Coast. These cities include San Francisco with 12.5 percent, Seattle with 12.7 percent, Minneapolis with 13.9 percent, and Portland with 15.3 percent. Three of the four cities with the highest percent of population between the

ages of 5 to 17 in 1980 were found in Texas. The cities with the
highest percent for 1980 include El Paso with 25.9 percent, Newark
with 25.4 percent, San Antonio with 23.6 percent, and Corpus Christi
with 23.2 percent.

Cities with the smallest percent of population between the ages of
5 to 17 in 1990 did not cluster on the West Coast as they did in 1980,
but were split between the East and West Coasts. The cities with the
smallest percent of population between the ages of 5 to 17 in 1990
include Seattle with 10.8 percent, San Francisco with 11.2 percent,
Boston with 12.8 percent and Washington, D.C., with 13.1 percent. On
the other hand, the cities with the highest percent for 1990 did cluster in
the Southwest as they did in 1980. These cities include El Paso with
23.2 percent, Corpus Christi with 21.9 percent, Fresno with 21.7
percent, and Bakersfield with 20.9 percent.

Unemployment Rate

City-level research also associates the unemployment rate[9] with the
homicide epidemic. The mean unemployment rate for the sample of
cities decreased from 9.49 percent in 1980 to 6.8 percent in 1991.
These rates can be compared to the national unemployment rate to give
an idea of how well the cities in this sample represent the United States
overall. The national unemployment rate in 1980 was 7.1 percent and
by 1991 the rate had fallen to 6.8 percent (Bureau of Labor Statistics
2005)[10]. Although the cities in the sample data had slightly higher
unemployment rates overall than the national average in 1980, the 1990
data values do match.

The highest unemployment rate for both 1980 and 1991 was in
Detroit, where the rate changed from an astounding 20.3 percent to a
reduced (but still relatively high) level of 13.1 percent. The next
highest unemployment rates in 1980 joined Detroit in clustering in the
Northeast of the United States: Newark, Buffalo, and Cleveland all had
rates above 15 percent. The lowest rates in 1980 were found in the
South and Southwest with the three lowest rates hovering around a rate
of 5 percent: Oklahoma City with a rate of 4.7 percent, Austin with a
rate of 5 percent, Lexington with a rate of 5.1 percent and Raleigh with
a rate of 5.3 percent.

---

[9] The unemployment rate is based on the percent of the total civilian labor
force.
[10] Retrieved online at ftp://ftp.bls.gov/pub/suppl/empsit.cpseea1.txt

The unemployment picture from 1980 to 1991 does not change much for the cities with the highest values. The highest unemployment rates in 1991 were found in Detroit at 13.1 percent, Newark at 12.6 percent, Fresno at 11 percent and Miami at 10.7 percent. The cities with the lowest rate were again found in the South and the Southwest with the lowest rates found in Omaha at 3.2 percent, Lexington at 3.8 percent, Tucson at 3.9 percent and Raleigh at 4.1 percent.

Resource Deprivation

The next four variables shown in table 5.2 will be transformed into an index of resource deprivation for statistical analysis. This index includes the percent of the population that is black, the percent of female-headed households, the median income, and the percent of families living below the poverty line. However, to get an idea of the distributions of these variables, each will be discussed individually.

Percent Black

The first of the variables in the resource deprivation index shown in table 5.2 is the percent of the population that is black. The descriptive statistics in table 5.2 indicate that both the mean and the range values increased between 1980 and 1990, pointing to a pattern of increased percentage of black residents in these urban areas. The minimum and maximum values demonstrate the stark contrast between major cities for this variable.

The individual city-level values for 1980 show that a handful of cities had black populations of less than four percent and all of these cities are found in the Southwest. The four lowest scores include Mesa with only 1.21 percent, Anaheim with 1.24 percent, Albuquerque with 2.32 percent, and Arlington with 2.82 percent. Compare these extremely low rates with the rates for the cities with the highest values, each with black populations making up over half of their populations: Washington, D.C., with 70.24 percent, Atlanta with 66.62 percent, Detroit with 63.03 percent, and Newark with 58.3 percent.

A decade later the percent of black residents increased in the overall sample, but the regions with the highest and lowest scores changed little. The four lowest scores were again found in the Southwest. The lowest scores were Mesa with 1.85 percent, Anaheim with 2.54 percent, Santa Ana with 2.62 percent, and Albuquerque 2.98 percent. The four highest scores also remained rather stable including

Detroit with 75.67 percent black, Atlanta with 67.07 percent, Washington, D.C., with 65.84 percent, and New Orleans with 61.92 percent. The fact that seven cities in the sample had populations that were more than half black and the 1990 value for Detroit, which indicates that the city was over three quarters black, are both indications of a pattern of an increasing percent of black residents in urban areas. The increasingly high percentage of black residents is important since prior research indicates that young black males were disproportionately affected by change in the homicide rates during the epidemic.

Female-Headed Households

The next variable in table 5.2 that is included in the resource deprivation index is the percent of female-headed households. While the range of scores for this variable is not as great as the percent black variable, quite a difference exists between the lowest and highest values. Individual city scores do not appear to group geographically at either the low end of the scale or the high end for this year. The four lowest scores include Arlington with 7.38 percent, Mesa 7.79 percent, Seattle with 9.11 percent and Aurora with 9.25 percent. The four highest scores tend to cluster around the Northeast. These cities include Newark with 28.31 percent, Detroit with 22.54 percent, Atlanta with 21.89 percent, and Baltimore with 21.86 percent.

Overall the percent of female-headed households increased slightly by 1990. All but eight of the cities in the sample showed an increase. Like the values for the cities with the lowest levels of female-headed households in 1980, no clear geographic pattern exists for the lowest individual city values in 1990. The lowest values include Seattle with 8.64 percent, Mesa with 8.9 percent, Virginia Beach with 9.06 percent, and Arlington with 9.21 percent. Three out of four of the cities with the highest values are again found in the Northeast. The highest values include Detroit with 30.36 percent, Newark with 28.29 percent, Baltimore with 24.60 percent and New Orleans with 24.03 percent.

Median Income

The last two variables presented in table 5.2, and included in the resource deprivation index, are based on income levels. The first of these is median income, which provides a measure of what the families in the middle of the income spectrum make if all family incomes were listed in numerical order. The mean value of the sample and individual city scores can also be compared to the national median income for this variable to give an idea of how closely the sample cities match the overall median income. In 1979 the national median income was $19,917 (U. S. Department of Commerce 1983), a little higher than the mean for the sample cities, which was $18,862. In 1989 the national median was $30,056 (U. S. Department of Commerce 1994), a little over $3,000 higher than the mean for the sample cities. This shift indicates a pattern of decreasing income levels for central urban areas relative to the nation as a whole (a pattern that will also be reflected in the changing poverty levels that will be discussed next).

Three out of four of the cities with the lowest median incomes in 1979 are found in the Southeast. The cities with the lowest median incomes include Newark at $11,989, Miami at $13,355, Atlanta at $13,591, and New Orleans at $15,003. All four of the cities with the highest median incomes in 1979 are found in the Southwest. The cities with the highest median incomes include San Jose at $25,598, Arlington at $24,478 Aurora at $23,994 and Anaheim at $23,112. All of the cities in the sample increased in median income between the 1979 and the 1989 measures. However, although the lowest scores are found in the East, they are not grouped as closely as the lowest scores for 1979. The lowest scores for 1989 include Miami at $16,925, Cleveland at $17,822, New Orleans at $18,477, and Buffalo at $18,482. The highest scores on the other hand are found in the South, and especially the Southwest. The highest scores include San Jose at $46,206, Anaheim at $39,620, Virginia Beach at $36,271, and Santa Ana at $35,162.

Poverty Level

The final variable included in the index of resource deprivation is the percent of families below the poverty level. Census data uses a formula that takes the minimum cost of an adequate diet and multiplies this figure by three to determine poverty levels (Fisher 1997). The 1979 mean for the sample of cities is almost three percent higher than the national average, which was 9.6 percent (U. S. Department of Commerce 1983). The cities in the sample with the lowest poverty levels are all found in the Southwest. These cities include Arlington with 3.8 percent, Aurora with 4.1 percent, Anaheim with 6 percent, and Mesa with 6.2 percent. On the other hand, the cities with the highest poverty levels are found in the East. These cities include Newark with 29.9 percent, Atlanta with 23.7 percent, New Orleans with 21.8 percent and Miami with 19.9 percent. All but 13 cities experienced increases in the poverty level between 1979 and 1989. The mean for the sample cities surpassed the national mean of 10 for 1989 (U. S. Department of Commerce 1994).

The cities with the lowest poverty rates in 1989 are found primarily in the South and especially the Southwest. These cities include Virginia Beach with 4.3 percent, Arlington with 5.7 percent, Aurora with 6.1 percent, and San Jose with 6.5 percent. In contrast to the regional pattern seen in median income, the cities with the highest poverty rates in 1989 are found in Eastern half of the United States. These cities include Detroit with 29 percent, New Orleans with 27.3 percent, Miami with 25.7 percent, and Cleveland with 25.2 percent. While only one city had over a quarter of its population in poverty in 1979, four cities met this criterion in 1989, indicating a pattern of increased income inequality and greater levels of resource deprivation in central urban areas. One more hopeful sign is the fact that the maximum poverty rate fell from 29.9 percent in 1979 to 29 percent in 1989.

Proximity

I will now turn to a discussion of a few unconventional independent variables included in the statistical analysis, now that the review of the independent variables usually included in community level homicide research is complete. The unconventional variables include proximity to cocaine hub measures, which provide an indication of cocaine availability, the per capita number of police officers, and the average homicide rate 1979-1981. I begin the discussion with an outline of variables derived from the location of cocaine hubs.

Figure 5.4. Map of major cocaine hubs in the continental U.S.

The map above provides an idea of the major cocaine hubs throughout the United States. Major distribution hubs and major destination cities are identified by the circles. The proximity variables used in this book are based on the distance between the cities in the sample and cocaine hubs indicated by NIDA data and discussed in chapter 3. I use two permutations of this measure. The first is simply the distance between cities and the nearest cocaine hub measured in road miles (i.e., the distance a vehicle would travel between cities). The second is the number of cocaine hubs within 500 miles. A summary of the proximity variables is presented in table 5.4.

**Table 5.4. Sample Cities, Proximity to Nearest
Cocaine Hub, and Number of Hubs within 500 Miles**

City	Proximity to Hub	Number of Hubs within 500 Miles
Mobile	328.62	3
Mesa	389.58	2
Phoenix	0[1]	3
Tucson	116	3
Anaheim	26.23	4
Bakersfield	113.7	4
Fresno	181.78	3
Long Beach	24.55	5
Los Angeles	0	7
Oakland	0	6
Riverside	35.04	8
Sacramento	87.3	7
San Diego	98.42	8
San Francisco	10.65	6
San Jose	40.35	6
Santa Ana	8.37	6
Aurora	14.97	1
Colorado Springs	68.58	1
Denver	0	1
Washington, D.C	136.63	4
Jacksonville	141.31	4
Miami	0	4
St. Petersburg	23.31	4
Tampa	84.71	4
Atlanta	0	3
Chicago	0	4

---

[1] All cities with a zero score for the "proximity to hub" variable are
cocaine hubs.

**Table 5.4. Sample Cities, Proximity to Nearest
Cocaine Hub, and Number of Hubs within 500 Miles
(continued)**

City	Proximity to Hub	Number of Hubs within 500 Miles
Louisville	299.11	4
New Orleans	347.46	2
Baltimore	103	5
Boston	214.89	4
Detroit	0	4
Minneapolis	0	2
St. Paul	9.65	2
Kansas City	437.2	1
St. Louis	295.27	1
Omaha	378.79	2
Las Vegas	270.68	4
Newark	0	5
Albuquerque	447.18	4
Buffalo	76.22	6
New York City	0	5
Charlotte	244.16	1
Raleigh	281.01	3
Cincinnati	244.12	5
Cleveland	0	7
Columbus	143.63	5
Toledo	61.12	4
Oklahoma City	444.87	1
Tulsa	494.59	1
Portland	0	2
Philadelphia	0	4
Pittsburgh	132.99	6
Memphis	388.26	1

**Table 5.4. Sample Cities, Proximity to Nearest
Cocaine Hub, and Number of Hubs within 500 Miles
(continued)**

City	Proximity to Hub	Number of Hubs within 500 Miles
Nashville	248.22	2
Arlington	255.97	1
Austin	165.35	1
Corpus Christi	222.97	1
Dallas	239.35	1
El Paso	0	3
Fort Worth	261.13	1
Houston	0	1
San Antonio	197.23	1
Virginia Beach	270.5	3
Seattle	0	2
Milwaukee	93.59	4
Mean	**156.47**	**3.36**
Standard Deviation	**151.42**	**2.00**

The average distance to the nearest cocaine distribution hub is
156.47 miles. Sixteen cities in the sample are cocaine hubs. All of
these cities have a value of zero miles for the proximity to the nearest
hub variable. Another 16 cities are within 100 miles of a cocaine hub.
The cities the furthest from a cocaine hub include Wichita at 519.04
miles, Tulsa at 494.59 miles, Albuquerque at 447.18 miles, and
Oklahoma City at 444.87 miles. Of these four cities, only Albuquerque
experienced a homicide epidemic.

Table 5.4 presents the number of hubs within 500 miles. Wichita is
the only city in the sample that has no cocaine hubs within 500 miles.
Seventeen cities have only one hub within that distance. At the other
end of the spectrum, three cities have seven hubs within five hundred
miles and two cities, Riverside and San Diego, have eight hubs within

that distance. Most of the cities with one or fewer hubs within the 500-mile radius are isolated in the Central Midwest and parts of Texas. On the other hand, most of the cities with six or more hubs within that distance are found in heavily populated areas, especially in the Southwest.

Table 5.5. Epidemic Cities: Per Capita Police[1] at Year of Homicide Rate Incline and Year of Decline

City	Police at Incline	Police at Decline
Mobile	151.29	246.02
Anaheim	142.03	127.03
Bakersfield	167.34	137.48
Fresno	156.43	105.54
Long Beach	165.17	178.45
Los Angeles	213.16	221.26
Oakland	170.4	190.96
Riverside	135.91	131
San Diego	144.61	166.36
San Francisco	243.51	244.98
Washington, D.C	612.94	781.02
St. Petersburg	154.59	183.99
Atlanta	293.11	398.21
Chicago	406.23	432
Louisville	223.27	242.06
New Orleans	245.47	281.62
Baltimore	379.38	402.06
Boston	336.67	344.6
Minneapolis	179.7	252.49
St. Paul	176.44	216.24
Kansas City	245.29	262.94
St. Louis	359.89	374.11
Las Vegas	223.54	200.41

---

[1] Per capita numbers were calculated by taking the total number of sworn officers in a city, dividing by the city population, and then multiplying by 100,000.

Table 5.5. Epidemic Cities: Per Capita Police at Year of Homicide Rate Incline and Year of Decline (continued).

City	Police at Incline	Police at Decline
Albuquerque	144.65	209.73
New York City	362.93	365.39
Charlotte	187.78	213.47
Cleveland	311.23	320.75
Columbus	216.2	223.32
Toledo	217.36	212.81
Philadelphia	424.28	419.47
Pittsburgh	285.86	317.97
Dallas	208.64	277.82
El Paso	139	153.29
San Antonio	155.07	168.57
Milwaukee	326.03	297.8
Mean Value	**243.01**	**265.75**
Standard Deviation	**263.83**	**290.41**

Police Officers

Table 5.5 presents the data on the per capita number of police officers[11] at the year of upturn of the epidemic and the year of downturn and the percent change in the per capita number of officers for the 33 cities that experienced the epidemic. I calculated the per capita numbers by dividing the total number of sworn officers for each city by the population of the city and then multiplying by 100,000. The cities with the fewest per capita number of police in the year the epidemic began are all in the Southwest. These cities include Riverside with 136 police per 100,000 residents, El Paso with 139 police per 100,000 residents, Anaheim with 142 police per 100,000 residents, and San Diego 145 police per 100,000 residents. However, the cities with the highest

---

[11] The variable "police officers" refers to sworn officers only, not civilians working for law enforcement.

number of police per 100,000 residents are found mainly in the Northeast. These cities include Washington D.C., with 613 police per 100,000 residents, Philadelphia with 424 police per 100,000 residents, Chicago with 406 police per 100,000 residents, and Baltimore with 379 police per 100,000 residents.

The cities with the lowest number of police per 100,000 residents in the year the epidemic ended for each are all found in California. These cities include Fresno with 106 police per 100,000 residents, Anaheim with 127 police per 100,000 residents, Riverside with 131 police per 100,000 residents, and Bakersfield with 138 police per 100,000 residents. The cities with the fewest police per 100,000 residents for the end of the epidemic are found on the West Coast. On the other hand, the cities with the highest number of police per 100,000 residents are found mainly in the Northeast. The cities with the highest number of police per 100,000 residents in the year the epidemic ended for each include Washington, D.C., with 781 police per 100,000 residents, Chicago with 432 police per 100,000 residents, Philadelphia with 420 police per 100,000 residents, and Baltimore with 402 police per 100,000 residents.

**Table 5.6. Non-Epidemic Cities, Per Capita Police[12]
in 1980 and 1990**

City	Police 1980	Police 1990
Mesa	163.70	137.46
Phoenix	209.86	197.27
Tucson	172.24	186.73
Sacramento	184.30	168.40
San Jose	126.73	142.15
Santa Ana	139.99	131.75
Aurora	171.25	171.99
Colorado Springs	157.99	141.92
Denver	284.68	278.44
Jacksonville	175.20	189.73
Miami	204.93	301.21
Tampa	193.52	302.84
Indianapolis	194.28	203.50
Wichita	142.11	146.38
Lexington	165.45	170.83
Detroit	347.94	438.53
Omaha	172.57	180.47
Newark	281.73	388.78
Buffalo	303.04	313.60
Raleigh	206.41	199.57
Cincinnati	260.24	263.43
Oklahoma City	180.54	198.33
Tulsa	187.48	190.31
Portland	179.46	180.35
Memphis	187.61	225.94

---

[12] Per capita numbers were calculated by taking the total number of
sworn officers in a city, dividing by the city population, and then
multiplying by 100,000.

**Table 5.6. Non-Epidemic Cities, Per Capita Police
in 1980 and 1990 (continued).**

City	Police 1980	Police 1990
Nashville	222.55	198.97
Arlington	124.08	133.73
Austin	157.82	164.94
Corpus Christi	133.93	143.72
Fort Worth	180.83	212.90
Houston	197.10	251.69
Virginia Beach	148.84	158.24
Seattle	210.61	244.84
Mean Value	**193.00**	**210.88**
Standard Deviation	**50.77**	**70.89**

Table 5.6 presents data on per capita number of police for 1980 and 1990 for the 33 cities that did not experience the epidemic. The ten-year length of time represented in this table is a little longer than the mean length of time between the year of upturn and year of downturn for epidemic cities, which was 8.26 years. Similar to the per capita number of police for the year of upturn for epidemic cities, the cities with the fewest police per 100,000 residents in 1980 are all found in the Southwestern states of California and Texas. These cities include Arlington with 124 police per 100,000 residents, San Jose with 127 police per 100,000 residents, Corpus Christi with 134 police per 100,000 residents, and Santa Ana with 140 police per 100,000 residents. Mirroring the epidemic cities for year of upturn, the non-epidemic cities with the highest number of police per 100,000 residents in 1980 are mainly in the Northeast. These cities include Detroit with 348 police per 100,000 residents, Buffalo with 303 police per 100,000 residents, Denver with 285 police per 100,000 residents, and Newark with 282 police per 100,000 residents.

Average Homicide Rate

The final independent variable I include in statistical tests is a measure of the average homicide rate. This variable was calculated by adding the homicide rates for each city from 1979-1981 and then dividing by three. This variable is included to test the effects of the general homicide rate prior to the onset of the epidemic. The level of homicide rate before the onset of an epidemic is a possible component for homicide rate change and the spread of homicide rate increases. Averaging over three years helps to insure that this variable represents the general homicide rate before the epidemic and not a single score, which could be an outlier.

Table 5.2 presents the mean, standard deviation, and minimum and maximum scores for this variable. The mean homicide rate is 19.47 for the sample with a standard deviation of 12.12. The range can be calculated with the minimum and maximum scores and with a range of 50.76 this measure has a high level of dispersion.

Cities with the lowest average homicide rates include Mesa with a rate of 3.02, Virginia Beach with a rate of 4.27, St. Paul with a rate of 5.58, Aurora with a rate of 6.39. No clear geographical pattern emerges among the low end of these scores. At the other end of the spectrum, the cities with the highest average homicide rates include Miami with a rate of 53.78, St. Louis with a rate of 53.56, Atlanta with a rate of 47.98, and Newark with a rate of 46.20. Again, no clear geographic pattern emerges for the highest scores for average homicide rate.

Summary for Independent Variables

What does the presentation of the variable characteristics above reveal for the analysis of the homicide epidemic characteristics? This summary briefly considers each of the variables enumerated above and indicates what the distribution of the variable values indicates in regard to the overarching issues addressed in this book.

The values of the population variable indicate a wide range of scores from the largest American cites which have at least several million residents to cities with populations that only hover above 250,000. The benefit of this range of cities is that statistical analysis will reveal whether patterns in homicide rate change are tied only to the largest cities or whether other large cities experienced the epidemic in concert. Interestingly, among the cities in the sample a significant fluctuation of population values occurs in both directions (some cities increasing in population and others losing population). These changes may prove influential for the changes in the homicide epidemic variables. Neither the cities with the greatest populations nor the cities with the least populations in the sample have any clear geographical pattern.

The next variable considered in the section above is population density. The values for this variable were similar both in terms of the values and the ranking of cities with the highest and lowest values. In this case, the Northeast and Southwest Coasts have the most densely populated cities, with the less densely populated cities sprinkled throughout the country. Since population density is a significant predictor of the vanguard cities for the incline and decline of the homicide epidemic (Messner et al, 2005), notice that the most densely populated cities are found on the coasts. This fact is especially interesting considering Blumstein's coastal hypothesis that indicates a coastal gradient for the start and end of the homicide epidemic (1995).

The next variable discussed above is the percent of city population aged 5-17. The proportion of young people is an important variable for the homicide epidemic, since the increase in homicide rates disproportionately affected this group (see e.g., Cook and Laub 1998). This variable has some interesting geographic distributions. For example in 1980 before the homicide epidemic took hold, three of the four cities with the smallest percent of youth were found along the West Coast. Additionally, Texas had three of the four cities with the largest percent of the youth. The Southwestern United States is a major funnel for cocaine into the United States. The concentration of young people in this corridor may have implications for the diffusion of the homicide epidemic. The pattern for the highest percent of young people remained relatively stable comparing 1980 and 1990, with Southwestern cities again topping the list.

The distribution of the unemployment rates is quite different from the percent young. For example, in 1980 the highest rates of unemployment were found in the Northeast, while the lowest rates were found in the South and Southwest. This general geographic pattern for unemployment rates remained for 1990 values. The range for unemployment rates is quite substantial for the cities in the sample. The city with the highest unemployment had a rate approximately four times the rate of the city with the lowest unemployment in both 1980 and 1990. If high unemployment is linked to greater participation in the crack market, then the cities in the South and Southwest with low unemployment may have received a buffering effect from increased homicide rates because the unemployed population was a smaller proportion of their overall city populations. On the other hand, cities in the Northeast may have been especially susceptible to crack market participation and the homicide rate increases that followed since these cities had a larger proportion of unemployed citizens.

The index of resource deprivation discussed above consists of four variables: the percent of black residents, the percent of female-headed households, the median income, and the poverty level. The reason the index is used for statistical tests, instead of the individual variables, is that these variables tend to be highly collinear and so the lists of cities with the highest and lowest values for each of these variables are similar. The cities with the most favorable values for each of the variables that make up the resource deprivation index are found primarily in the Southwest. The cities with the least favorable values tend to group in the East and along the East Coast. This notion is interesting considering that the Southwest is a major route into the United States for cocaine, and many of the major East Coast cities with the highest levels of resource deprivation are cocaine destination cities. Again, like unemployment, if high levels of resource deprivation are linked to an increase in crack market activity, then the Southwest appears to have some level of protection from this type of activity, while many cities in the East may be highly susceptible to the emergence of violent crack markets.

The statistical analysis includes two measures based on the proximity of cities to cocaine hubs: the distance to the nearest cocaine hub and the number of cocaine hubs within 500 miles. These proximity variables have not been included in any tests on the homicide epidemic before this study. The cocaine hubs on which these measures are based are found primarily in port cities ringing the coasts and international borders. A high concentration of cocaine hubs is also found in the Northeast.

The policing variable used in the statistical analysis is the per capita number of police. This variable is key for a number of reasons. First, the police are charged with reducing crime rates and reducing fear of crime (although the actual effects of policing on these variables is debatable). Second, out of all of the independent variables, policing is the only one that has the potential to adapt to increasing homicide levels with increased intensity and innovative tactics. In summary, policing is a relatively malleable variable, while demographic characteristics, for example, cannot be greatly altered in the face of increasing crime.

The range of policing levels is quite high for cities in the sample under investigation. Cities with the lowest number of per capita police officers have levels of police per 100,000 people in the 100s, while cities with the highest numbers have police in the 400s or even greater levels. This variation in the sample provides a wide spectrum of policing, which will help determine what levels of policing might deter the diffusion of homicide.

Dependent Variables

This book considers three major characteristics of the city-level homicide epidemic as dependent variables. They are:

1. The presence of the epidemic. Did a city experience a homicide epidemic during the period of time under consideration or not?

2. The magnitude of the epidemic. This variable is measured in two ways. First, the absolute change in magnitude, or the difference in raw city homicide rates from the first year of the epidemic until the last year of the epidemic period. Second, the percent change in magnitude, or percent of change in city homicide rates from the first year of the epidemic until the last year of the epidemic period.

3. The duration of the epidemic. This variable is measured by the number of years the epidemic lasted from the first year of the epidemic until the last year of the epidemic period. A reversal in the direction of the fitted homicide rate from an inclining rate to a declining rate marks the end of the epidemic.

The next section considers each of these variables. This review will serve several purposes. First, the review will identify individual cities that have measurements that stand out for each of the three main dependent variables. Second, the review will highlight the range of scores for the sample. Finally, the review will allow the sample values to be compared with the overall national homicide epidemic characteristics.

Presence

The presence variable simply refers to whether a city experienced an epidemic in the window of time under consideration (see the discussion on the technical definition of an epidemic in chapter 4). Thirty-five of the sixty-eight cities in the sample experienced a homicide epidemic during this period of time based on the results of the spline regressions. Table 5.3 shows the dates of the year of upturn and year of downturn for the cities that experienced the epidemic and asterisks for the 33 cities that did not (see discussion on the four typical patterns followed by non-epidemic cities in chapter 4). The presence variable will be included in statistical tests to determine if significant differences exist for cities that did and did not experience the epidemic depending on the independent variables reviewed above.

Table 5.7. Epidemic Cities: Duration, Absolute Magnitude, and Percent Change in Homicide Rates

City	Absolute Magnitude	Percent Change in Rates	Duration
Mobile	8.28	52.27	13
Anaheim	6.12	104.26	11
Bakersfield	3.3	30.39	13
Fresno	7.73	60.11	13
Long Beach	11.6	76.62	7
Los Angeles	7.71	33.18	7
Oakland	13.92	45.52	8
Riverside	6.75	100.90	12
San Diego	5.38	57.91	7
San Francisco	4.99	41.97	6
Washington, D.C	58.01	270.70	5
St. Petersburg	8.7	112.26	6
Atlanta	31.58	112.87	7
Chicago	12.13	54.74	4
Louisville	8.95	68.01	11
New Orleans	52.88	176.50	10
Baltimore	21.74	83.87	10
Boston	6.36	40.10	1
Minneapolis	15.03	225.34	13
St. Paul	5.86	159.24	14
Kansas City	13.42	68.86	8
St. Louis	35.85	102.19	7
Las Vegas	6.77	55.40	11
Albuquerque	4.56	50.22	14
New York City	10.69	49.49	6
Charlotte	14.16	96.92	6
Cleveland	10.29	41.11	6
Columbus	5.8	44.14	7

Table 5.7. Epidemic Cities: Duration, Absolute Magnitude, and Percent Change in Homicide Rates (continued).

City	Absolute Magnitude	Percent Change in Rates	Duration
Toledo	4.9	62.58	9
Philadelphia	15.1	102.17	6
Pittsburgh	12.46	158.52	5
Dallas	18.82	65.08	8
El Paso	3.18	49.69	6
San Antonio	5.03	27.04	5
Milwaukee	17.97	228.92	7
Mean Value	**13.60**	**88.83**	**8.26**
Standard Deviation	**12.54**	**59.21**	**3.05**

Magnitude

Table 5.7 includes the values and descriptive statistics for the absolute magnitude of the homicide epidemic for cities that experienced the epidemic, as well as the percent change in rates. The change in homicide rates from the beginning of the epidemic period to the end of the epidemic period for each city determines these variables. For the absolute magnitude variable, the mean value is 13.6 with a standard deviation of 12.54, revealing a high degree of variation. The cities with the highest values include Washington, D.C., with a change in rates of 58.01, New Orleans with a change in rates of 52.88, St. Louis with a change in rates of 35.85 and Atlanta with a change in rates of 31.58. These cities have no clear geographic relationship.

On the other hand, a geographic pattern emerges among the lowest values with high representation in the Southwest. The lowest values include El Paso with a change in rates of 3.18, Bakersfield with a change in rates of 3.3, Albuquerque with a change of 4.56, and Toledo with a change of 4.9.

The percent change in homicide rates demonstrates even greater variation than the absolute magnitude variable. In this case, the values range from the lowest score of 27.04 percent change in rates for San Antonio to the highest score of 270.70 percent change in rates for Washington, D.C. The mean value for the overall sample of cities is 88.83. The standard deviation is 59.21 highlighting the high level of variability for this measure. While discovering that Washington, D.C., has the highest percent change in homicide rates, is no surprise, notice that the other cities with changes in their homicide rates over 200 percent are Minneapolis with a 225.34 percent change and Milwaukee with a 228.92 percent change. These are two Midwestern cities whose homicide epidemics have drawn less notice. Another interesting finding is that the homicide epidemic in Washington, D.C., was highly intense and relatively short. Washington, D.C. presents a pattern that hints at an inverse relationship between the duration and the magnitude of the epidemic period.

Just as in the case of the change in absolute magnitude, the highest values have no clearly apparent geographical pattern. A geographic pattern appears to occur among cities with the lowest percent change in rates, with high representation in the Southwest. The lowest values include San Antonio with a percent change of 27.04, Bakersfield with a percent change of 30.39, Los Angeles with a percent change of 33.18, and Boston with a percent change of 40.10.

Duration

Table 5.7 presents a summary of the duration variable. The duration variable ranges widely from the shortest epidemic period of one year for Boston[13] to the cities with the longest epidemic periods of 14 years for Albuquerque and St. Paul. Notice that these two cities with the longest durations are neither coastal cities, nor the mega-cities that have received the greatest attention focused on the national homicide epidemic (e.g., Blumstein 1995). Table 5.7 presents the descriptive statistics for the duration variable. The cities in this sample that experienced a homicide epidemic had a mean epidemic period that lasted 8.26 years with a standard deviation of 3.05 years. These

---

[13] While it may be questionable that a single year of an upturn in rates can be termed an epidemic period, it does meet the criteria for an epidemic outlined for this book. Only one city has a single year epidemic, while the next lowest value for the duration variable is four years.

descriptive statistics can be compared to the homicide rate duration for the national epidemic that lasted five years from 1987, when the rate was 8.3, to 1991, when the rate was 9.8 (U.S. Department of Justice 2004).

The relationship between the duration of the epidemic and the magnitude deserves attention. While El Paso and Washington, D.C., represent the two most extreme values for absolute magnitude, they only differ by one year in the duration of their epidemic period, and both are below the mean for the length of their epidemic periods. No clear geographical pattern for the high or low values for the cities emerges in the sample and there is also no clear pattern between the duration and the magnitude measures. The next section presents the results of correlation tests that will reveal the extent to which the variables are correlated.

Summary for Dependent Variables

The examination of the values and descriptive statistics for the dependent variables reveals some interesting findings. First, considering the presence variable, around half of the cities in the sample experienced the epidemic during the period under investigation. Messner et al. (2005) point out the fact that a high proportion of large U.S. cities experienced the epidemic. One of the key goals of this study is to examine characteristics of both cities that experienced the epidemic and cities that did not. Second, the two permutations of the magnitude variable reveal a couple of interesting findings. No clear geographical pattern emerges for cities with the highest values. On the other hand, a pattern for cities with the lowest values emerged with high representation of cities in the Southwest.

The mean value for the duration variable reveals that, on average, the epidemic lasted longer for the cities in the sample than the national homicide epidemic. Notice that this measure demonstrates a significant level of variability. Some cities experienced relatively short epidemics and at the other end of the scale, a couple of cities experienced epidemics that lasted almost three times longer than the duration of the national epidemic.

Correlation Results

Now that I have reviewed the descriptive statistics and univariate characteristics of the independent and dependent variables, I will discuss the results of correlation tests. Bivariate correlations are useful for understanding how closely the values of variables are aligned and the form of a relationship (e.g., positive or negative) if the variables are correlated. The correlations provide a preliminary look at the relationships between the variables.

Another reason for conducting correlation tests is to uncover any collinearity among the variables. If two variables are highly collinear the regression coefficients of the independent variables will have inflated standard errors, which means that accurate estimation of the coefficients is not possible (Gujarati 1995: 322). The general rule is that a correlation coefficient (Pearson's r) of 0.8 or greater between two variables is evidence of high collinearity.

Since overall collinearity depends on the strength of the multiple correlations between independent variables, I have also tested the variance inflation factor (VIF) for the independent variables. The general rule is that the VIF should not exceed 10 (Belsely, Kuh, and Welsch 1980). All of the independent variables tested had a VIF of less than four, indicating that the inflation of parameter estimates associated with high levels of collinearity is not problematic. The next section reviews the correlation coefficients for the independent variables and then the dependent variables for the magnitude and duration measures[14].

---

[14] The correlation between the epidemic presence and the other dependent variables will not be included since the results of such correlations cannot be interpreted.

Table 5.8. Correlations for Independent Variables Used with the presence of the homicide epidemic, N=68.

Correlations for Independent Variables Used with Presence								
Variable	Pop.	Density	Young	Unemp.	Deprivation	Proximity	Count	Police
Population (Probability)	1	0.65 (<.0001)	-0.03 (0.7960)	0.09 (0.4803)	0.19 (0.1227)	-0.26 (0.0313)	0.18 (0.1451)	0.39 (0.0011)
Density (Probability)		1	-0.26 (0.0316)	0.37 (0.0017)	0.47 (<.0001)	-0.41 (0.0004)	0.39 (0.0009)	0.65 (<.0001)
Percent Young (Probability)			1	0.08 (0.5399)	-0.01 (0.9120)	0.06 (0.6189)	-0.09 (0.4564)	-0.38 (0.0016)
Unemployment (Probability)				1	0.55 (<.0001)	-0.34 (0.0048)	0.51 (<.0001)	0.38 (0.0013)
Deprivation (Probability)					1	-0.16 (0.1836)	0.21 (0.0876)	0.67 (<.0001)
Proximity (Probability)						1	-0.49 (<.0001)	-0.21 (0.0883)
Proximity Count (Probability)							1	0.17 (0.1682)

Independent Variables

Table 5.8 presents the Pearson's r values for the relationships between the independent variables used in tests on the presence of the epidemic. In this case the logged population, the logged density, the percent young, unemployment, and the resource deprivation index measures are from around 1980. The 1980 predates the initiation of the national homicide epidemic and the years in which the epidemic began for major U.S. cities (Messner et al. 2005). The per capita number of police is from the year of incline for cities that experienced the epidemic and from 1980 for cities that did not experience the epidemic. The averaged homicide rate is the mean homicide rate from 1979-1981 for each city.

The population variable is significantly correlated with five other variables at the .05 level. Four of these are positive correlations: population density, resource deprivation, police per capita, and the averaged homicide rate. This means that cities with large populations are also more likely to have high rates of these other variables. On the other hand, proximity to the nearest cocaine hub is negatively correlated with population, which means that the larger a city is the closer it is to a cocaine hub (or the more likely it is to be a cocaine hub).

Population density is significantly correlated with seven variables. Five of these are positive correlations: unemployment, resource deprivation, the number of cocaine hubs within 500 miles, the police per capita, and the averaged homicide rate. Proximity and the percent young are both negatively correlated with density. This means that generally, the denser a city's population is, the smaller the youth cohort. No other significant relationships emerge for the percent young.

The unemployment rate is significantly positively correlated with five of the remaining variables: resource deprivation, the number of cocaine hubs within 500 miles, the police per capita, and the averaged homicide rate. Proximity to the nearest cocaine hub is the lone significant negative correlation.

Resource deprivation is significantly positively correlated with two of the remaining variables: per capita police and the averaged homicide rate. Proximity is significantly negatively correlated with the number of cocaine hubs within 500 miles. Finally, the per capita number of police is positively correlated with the averaged homicide rate, indicating the higher the per capita number of police, the higher the general homicide rate prior to the homicide epidemic.

Many of the independent variables with values from circa 1980 are significantly correlated with other independent variables. However, none of the relationships are strong enough to prohibit the inclusion of both variables in multivariate analysis. Most of these relationships are not particularly surprising. Urban crime theory indicates that large, densely populated cities have relatively high levels of unemployment and resource deprivation (see e.g., Wilson 1987 and 1996). The smaller percentage of youth in large, dense cities is somewhat surprising, although this could be due to a higher rate of abortions in urban areas (Donahue and Levitt 2001).

Table 5.9. Correlations for Independent Variables Used with the magnitude and duration of the homicide epidemic, N=68.

Variable	Pop.	Density	Young	Unemp.	Deprivatio	Proximity	Count	Police
		Correlations for Independent Variables Used with Presence						
Population (Probability)	1							
Density (Probability)	0.63 (<.0001)	1						
Percent Young (Probability)	-0.05 (0.6810)	-0.28 (0.0197)	1					
Unemployment (Probability)	0.19 (0.1207)	0.39 (0.0010)	0.36 (0.0029)	1				
Deprivation (Probability)	0.09 (0.4850)	0.26 (0.0335)	0.14 (0.2672)	0.56 (<.0001)	1			
Proximity (Probability)	-0.26 (0.0314)	-0.44 (0.0002)	0.05 (0.7014)	-0.37 (0.0019)	-0.1 (0.4009)	1		
Count (Probability)	0.19 (0.1276)	0.44 (0.0002)	-0.09 (0.4897)	0.36 (0.0028)	0.09 (0.4529)	-0.49 (<.0001)	1	
Police (Probability)	0.5 (<.0001)	0.5 (<.0001)	-0.31 (0.0108)	0.31 (0.0112)	0.62 (<.0001)	-0.16 (0.1956)	0.11 (0.3592)	

Table 5.9 presents the correlation values for the independent variables used in tests on the magnitude and duration of the epidemic. Logged population, logged density, the percent young, unemployment, and the resource deprivation index measures are from around 1990. The1990 date predates the end of the national homicide epidemic and the years in which the epidemic ended for major U.S. cities (Messner et al. 2005)[15]. The per capita number of police is from the year of decline for cities that experienced the epidemic and from 1990 for cities that did not experience the epidemic. The averaged homicide rate is the mean homicide rate from 1979-1981 for each city. The correlation coefficients, direction of relationships, and significance of relationships are largely consistent with the relationships seen in table 5.8. Two notable changes emerge concerning significance. Population size is positively correlated with resource deprivation and the percent young is no longer significantly correlated with the unemployment rate or the per capita police.

Table 5.10. Correlation Coefficients for Magnitude and Duration Variables

Variable	Duration	Absolute Magnitude	Percent Change in Homicide Rates
Duration	1	-.15207	0.06938
(Probability)		(0.3832)	(0.6921)
Absolute Magnitude		1	0.64173
(Probability)			(<.0001)

N=35 for all correlations

Dependent Variables

Table 5.10 presents the correlations coefficients and significance levels for the relationships between the magnitude measures and the duration of the homicide epidemic for cities that experienced the epidemic. The correlation values reveal to what extent the magnitude variables vary with the duration of the epidemic. This step helps to address an important issue on the form of the epidemic. Magnitude measures

---

[15] The lone exception is St. Petersburg, where the epidemic ended in 1989. For St. Petersburg, the social variables are from circa 1980.

negatively related to the duration measure suggest that epidemic patterns that are more intense (i.e., higher homicide rate change) burn out more quickly, than less intense epidemics, which may continue on for a longer time. On the other hand, magnitude measures positively related to the duration suggest either highly intense epidemics that lasted many years, or relatively less intense epidemics that lasted fewer years.

Table 5.10 shows that only the magnitude measures are significantly correlated. The duration variable is significantly correlated with neither the absolute magnitude nor the percent change in magnitude. The correlation coefficients indicate no clear relationship between the variation in duration and the variation in magnitude.

Bivariate Tests

This section reviews the results of bivariate statistical tests. This step provides a preliminary idea about the relationships between the independent variables and the dependent variables. The results of the multiple regression tests reveals which variables are the best predictors of each of the dependent variables. However, since bivariate tests are frequently included as evidence in support of hypotheses (e.g., Messner et al. 2005), a short review before continuing on to the multivariate analysis is worthwhile.

Table 5.11. Bivariate Logistic Regressions on Presence of the Homicide Epidemic

Variable	Estimate	Standard Error	Probability *	N
Population (Logged)	0.74	0.39	0.03	68
Density (Logged)	1.08	0.39	<0.01	68
Resource Deprivation	0.31	0.16	0.02	68
Unemploy-ment	0.11	0.09	0.10	68
Percent Young	-0.09	0.10	0.19	68
Per Capita Police	<0.01	<0.01	0.04	68
Distance to the Nearest Cocaine Hub	<0.01	<0.01	0.19	68
Number of Hubs within 500 Miles	0.33	0.14	0.01	68
Averaged Homicide Rate	0.04	0.02	0.03	68

*All probability results are for one-tailed tests based on hypotheses.

<u>Presence</u>

Table 5.11 shows the results of bivariate logistic regressions between each of the main independent variables and the presence of the homicide epidemic. Population size, population density, resource deprivation, the number of police per capita, the number of cocaine hubs within 500 miles, and the averaged homicide rate are each significant at the .05 level and each of these relationships is positive.

Table 5.12. Bivariate Regressions on Absolute Magnitude of the Homicide Epidemic

Variable	Estimate	Standard Error	Probability *	N
Population (Logged)	-2.37	2.82	0.20	68
Density (Logged)	-5.73	2.96	0.03	68
Resource Deprivation	1.20	1.14	0.15	68
Unemploy-ment	-1.76	0.99	0.04	68
Percent Young	-0.13	0.84	0.44	68
Per Capita Police	<-0.01	<0.01	0.15	68
Distance to the Nearest Cocaine Hub	-0.02	0.01	0.09	68
Number of Hubs within 500 Miles	-2.85	0.98	<0.01	68
Averaged Homicide Rate	0.16	0.16	0.17	68

*All probability results are for one-tailed tests based on hypotheses.

Absolute Magnitude

Table 5.12 shows the results of bivariate regressions between each of the independent variables and the absolute magnitude of the homicide epidemic. Of all the independent variables only the population density, unemployment and the number of cocaine hubs within 500 miles are significant at the .05 level. Each of these relationships is negative.

**Table 5.13. Bivariate Regressions on Percent Change in
Magnitude of the Homicide Epidemic**

Variable	Estimate	Standard Error	Probability *	N
Population (Logged)	-14.26	10.86	0.10	68
Density (Logged)	0.81	12.17	0.48	68
Resource Deprivation	4.43	4.92	0.19	68
Unemploy-ment	-9.27	4.20	0.02	68
Percent Young	-5.24	3.33	0.06	68
Per Capita Police	-0.00	0.00	0.16	68
Distance to the Nearest Cocaine Hub	-0.05	0.06	0.20	68
Number of Hubs within 500 Miles	-7.59	4.26	0.04	68
Averaged Homicide Rate	-0.63	0.70	0.18	68

*All probability results are for one-tailed tests based on hypotheses.

Percent Change in Magnitude

Table 5.13 shows the results of bivariate regressions between each of
the independent variables and the percent change in magnitude of the
homicide epidemic. Of all the independent variables only
unemployment and the number of cocaine hubs within 500 miles are
significant at the .05 level. Both of these relationships are negative.

Table 5.14. Bivariate Regressions on Duration of the Homicide Epidemic

Variable	Estimate	Standard Error	Probability *	N
Population (Logged)	-4.54	1.97	0.01	68
Density (Logged)	-7.16	1.93	<0.01	68
Resource Deprivation	-1.65	0.82	0.02	68
Unemployment	-1.61	0.70	0.01	68
Percent Young	0.65	0.61	0.14	68
Per Capita Police	<-0.01	<0.01	0.01	68
Distance to the Nearest Cocaine Hub	-0.01	0.01	0.10	68
Number of Hubs within 500 Miles	-1.85	0.72	<0.01	68
Averaged Homicide Rate	-0.26	0.12	0.02	68

*All probability results are for one-tailed tests based on hypotheses.

Duration

Table 5.14 shows the results of bivariate regressions between each of the independent variables and the duration of the homicide epidemic. Population size, population density, resource deprivation, unemployment, the per capita number of police, the number of cocaine hubs within 500 miles, and the averaged homicide rate are all significant at the .05 level. All of these relationships are negative.

Multivariate Analysis

Although bivariate tests can reveal something about the relationship between variables, these tests cannot reveal how strong a relationship might be if the effects of other variables are controlled or which variables are the most important predictors. Multivariate techniques allow for testing the relationships between variables controlling for the effects of other variables. Comparing different regressions reveals the best predictor variables. The following sections review the statistical analysis of the effects of the independent variables on the dependent variables.

First, I present the results of the multivariate logistic regressions with the presence variable as the dependent variable. Next, I present the results of the multivariate Tobit regressions for the magnitude measures and the duration variable. The results shown are the effects of the independent variables on the latent dependent variables, which means that the effects are for all of the cities in the sample and not just those that experienced the epidemic (see the discussion on Tobit regression in chapter 4). I present the results of statistical tests only for the unrestricted model (the model including all the independent variables) and the best-fitting model selected according to a conventional goodness-of-fit test. Of these, the best-fitting model is the most important for predicting the dependent variables. The unrestricted model is included only as a reference.

A number of statistical tests are available to determine which statistical model among competing models best fits the data. Goodness-of-fit tests are used to compare models to establish the relative value of including or excluding different independent variables. Following the logical principle of Occam's razor (and statistical rules pertaining to parsimony) a simple model is preferred over a more complex model. However, if a model with additional variables fits a dataset significantly better than a simpler model, then statistical analysis should include the additional parameters.

The relationship between the independent and dependent variables is unknown and a statistical model cannot be accepted *a priori*. Additionally, the theory guiding this book is not well fleshed out in terms of emphasizing the relationships between the independent and dependent variables. To explore the relationships I consider an array of models, before accepting one as the "true" model that provides the best fit.

I use Akaike's Information criterion (AIC), a standard test to ascertain the best-fitting model. I conducted the tests to determine the model that best fit the data with the following steps: first, I ran regressions for the effects of each of the independent variables on each of the dependent variables. Then, I ran regressions for the effects of every combination of independent variables on each of the dependent variables, in combinations of two, three, four, and so forth, until every possible combination of independent variables under investigation was considered. I determined the overall best-fitting model by comparing the Akaike's Information criterion (AIC) scores between each of the models. Following the theoretical expectations I also tested for the effects of the interaction between the cocaine hub variables and the independent variables. None of these interactions were significant, and they are not presented in the tables of results.

The entire list of models can be seen in appendix A. Appendix B shows the AIC scores for each of the models for the presence of the epidemic. Appendix C shows the AIC scores for each of the models for the absolute magnitude of the epidemic. Appendix D shows the AIC scores for each of the models for the percent change in magnitude. Appendix E shows the AIC scores for each of the models for the duration of the epidemic.

Chapter 3 includes a detailed discussion of hypothesis development, as well as an enumeration of the specific hypotheses that are the subject of the multiple regression tests. The hypotheses for the presence of the epidemic include the expectation of positive relationships for the following variables: population density, population size, resource deprivation, unemployment, percent young, and the number of cocaine hubs within 500 miles. On the other hand, I predict negative relationships for the number of police and the proximity variable.

Table 5.15. Logistic Regression Coefficients for Presence of Homicide Epidemic: Unrestricted Model (Model A) and Best-fitting Model (Model B)

Variables	Model A	Model B
Intercept	2.31	-8.79**
(Standard Error)	(13.43)	(3.20)
Density (logged)	0.96	1.08**
(Standard Error)	(0.62)	(0.39)
Population (Logged)	-0.81	--
(Standard Error)	(0.96)	--
Resource Deprivation	0.94	--
(Standard Error)	(0.52)	--
Unemployment	-0.12	--
(Standard Error)	(0.14)	--
Percent Young	-0.05	--
(Standard Error)	(0.13)	--
Proximity to Hub	<0.01	--
(Standard Error)	(<0.01)	--
Number of Hubs within 500 Miles	0.23	--
(Standard Error)	(0.21)	--
Average Homicide Rate	0.03	--
(Standard Error)	(0.04)	--
Per Capita Police	<0.01	--
(Standard Error)	(<0.01)	--
N	68	68

-- Variable omitted
* $p < .05$
** $p < .01$

Presence

Table 5.15 presents the results of logistic regressions on the presence of the epidemic. Again, all of the independent social variables are values from circa 1980. See the discussion in chapter 4 for a detailed explanation of the timing of the values.

Table 5.15 presents two models, their regression coefficients, and their standard errors. Model A includes city population (logged), city density (logged), the resource deprivation index, the unemployment rate, the percent of the population age 5 to17, the proximity to nearest cocaine hub, number of cocaine hubs within 500 miles, the averaged homicide rate 1979-81, and the per capita number of police. The goodness-of-fit model selection techniques discussed above indicate that the best-fitting model for the prediction of the presence of the homicide epidemic is the model that only includes logged population density. The statistical results for this model are shown in table 5.15 as Model B. City population density (logged) is positively related to the presence of the epidemic with a coefficient of 1.08.

Unexpectedly, the best-fitting statistical model for predicting whether or not a city experienced a homicide epidemic is the model that only includes population density. Surprisingly, the cocaine measures were not identified as important predictors, contrary to Blumstein's assumptions about the role of cocaine in promoting the onset of the epidemic. Apparently, density plays a key role in the diffusion of violent behavior. Although testing the micro-level path of homicide diffusion is beyond the scope of this book, the importance of density may be incorporated into the nascent theoretical work on the homicide epidemic.

Possibly the diffusion of violence occurs more readily in densely populated cities than in cities that are less densely populated. As violent behavior increases, people may arm themselves and take other defensive measures that may decrease social control in public areas and increase the likelihood of deadly disputes. This process may be more pronounced in areas in which people live in close proximity to each other, since violent behavior is more likely to intimately involve a greater number of people. For example, a shooting in a densely populated apartment complex is likely to cause behavioral change in a greater number of people than someone shot in the outskirts of a town in less populated area.

Cohen and Tita (1999) use exploratory spatial data analysis (ESDA) to look at the potential of a contagious diffusion of youth gang homicide during the epidemic. They found evidence of contagious diffusion in the peak year of the epidemic, but in other years, the increase in homicides was simultaneous in different neighborhoods (including in census tracts that did not adjoin). How far the influence of a series of violent acts may spread is unclear. In the next chapter, I discuss in greater detail how density could have contributed to community environments, making them more susceptible to the homicide epidemic.

<u>Magnitude</u>

The next series of statistical results are derived not from logistic regression, as was the case for the presence variable, but instead from statistical techniques for data that contain some censored values. These techniques are commonly used for survival analysis and accelerated time failure, but can be used for a broad range of purposes where data values are censored. The statistical formulas and technical details of this approach are discussed in chapter 3, but here I review what these techniques provide substantively to the remaining dependent variables.

Since not all cities experienced the homicide epidemic, not all cities have valid response data for the magnitude and duration measures. In this case, these variables are called "censored" since they are "cut off" for cities that were vulnerable to the epidemic, but never actually experienced it. If these cities are not included in regression analysis, then the results are biased. Procedures developed for censored data allow the estimation of parameters by maximum likelihood using an algorithm that includes information from the entire set of subjects (in this case cities), not just those that have values for the dependent variables. The regression coefficients are for the latent absolute magnitude variable and account for the effects of the independent variables on all cities in the sample. I first discuss the results of the application of these techniques for the magnitude measures and then go on to discuss the duration variable.

Table 5.16. Regression Coefficients for the Effects of the Independent Variables on the Latent Absolute Magnitude Variable: Unrestricted Model (Model A) and Best-fitting Model (Model B)

Variables	Model A	Model B
Intercept	84.24	32.69**
(Standard Error)	(68.24)	(4.23)
Density (logged)	-3.51	--
(Standard Error)	(3.86)	--
Population (Logged)	-0.67	--
(Standard Error)	(4.16)	--
Resource Deprivation	1.94	--
(Standard Error)	(2.85)	--
Unemployment	-2.20	--
(Standard Error)	(1.30)	--
Percent Young	-0.28	--
(Standard Error)	(0.94)	--
Proximity to Hub	0.01	--
(Standard Error)	(0.02)	--
Number of Hubs within 500 Miles	-1.93	-2.85**
(Standard Error)	(1.12)	(0.98)
Average Homicide Rate	0.22	--
(Standard Error)	(0.22)	--
Per Capita Police	<0.01	--
(Standard Error)	(<0.01)	--
N	68	68

-- Variable omitted
* $p < .05$
** $p < .01$

Table 5.16 presents the results of regressions on the latent absolute magnitude of variable. In this case, all of the independent variables (aside from the proximity measures and per capita number of police) are values from circa 1990 (except for St. Petersburg, since the epidemic ended there prior to 1990). None of the variables in Model A, the unrestricted model, are significant at the .05 level.

The best-fitting model includes only the number of cocaine hubs within 500 miles. However, the direction of the relationship is counter to the expected relationship. The negative relationship between number of cocaine hubs within 500 miles and the absolute magnitude indicates that the more cocaine hubs within 500 miles, the lower the absolute magnitude of the homicide epidemic. Since this is the opposite of the expected relationship, it requires a rethinking of the expectations guiding my hypothesis.

If the violence surrounding the crack market was exacerbated by market competition over control of territory and product, then it stands to reason that buyers with multiple options for cocaine sources will be able to secure cocaine more easily and more cheaply than buyers isolated in areas that have more limited access to sources. Increased access and lower cost could help to reduce the violent effects of competition since buyers would have an increased number of choices for their sources. Furthermore, the suppressed prices that multiple source points potentially offer could also reduce interest in dealing, since profit margins may also be reduced. Blumstein (1995) calls attention to the importance of the diffusion of crack cocaine on the homicide epidemic. However, this relationship appears to be moderated by the availability of cocaine.

Table 5.17. Regression Coefficients for the Effects of the Independent Variables on the Latent Percent Change in Magnitude Variable: Unrestricted Model (Model A) and Best-fitting Model (Model B)

Variables	Model A	Model B
Intercept	371.65	187.82**
(Standard Error)	(270.20)	(33.16)
Density (logged)	19.03	--
(Standard Error)	(16.36)	--
Population (Logged)	-17.97	--
(Standard Error)	(15.20)	--
Resource Deprivation	33.58**	10.56*
(Standard Error)	(11.13)	(4.93)
Unemployment	-9.15	-13.19**
(Standard Error)	(5.10)	(4.48)
Percent Young	-3.54	--
(Standard Error)	(4.11)	--
Proximity to Hub	0.04	--
(Standard Error)	(0.06)	--
Number of Hubs within 500 Miles	-8.22	--
(Standard Error)	(4.33)	--
Averaged Homicide Rate	-2.09*	--
(Standard Error)	(0.84)	--
Per Capita Police	<0.01	--
(Standard Error)	(<0.01)	--
N	68	68

-- Variable omitted
* p< .05
** p< .01

Table 5.17 presents the results of regressions on the latent percent change in magnitude variable. Again, the independent variables (aside from the proximity measures and the per capita number of police) are values from circa 1990 (except for St. Petersburg). The best-fitting model, seen in table 5.17 as Model B, includes resource deprivation and unemployment. The direction of the relationship for resource deprivation is positive, as expected. However, the direction of the relationship for unemployment is counter to the expected relationship. The negative relationship between unemployment and the percent change in magnitude indicates that the higher the unemployment rate, the lower the absolute magnitude of the homicide epidemic.

I interpret these findings with reference to the overarching theory guiding this book. High levels of resource deprivation could have lead to higher percent change in the magnitude of the homicide epidemic since cities with great resource deprivation are fertile grounds for the introduction of crack cocaine. For instance, the population of such areas has restricted access to legitimate job opportunities, mental health care, and recreational options. In turn, these factors may play a role in the choices people make for securing an income, self-medication, and seeking pleasure. Furthermore, such areas may have low levels of social control, which could, in turn, allow the proliferation of open drug sales and increase the likelihood of violent dispute resolution.

The negative relationship of the unemployment rate and the percent change in magnitude is somewhat surprising in light of the hypotheses presented in chapter 3. This finding contradicts the expectations of the hypothesis. How can this finding be explained? Remember that black markets do not operate in a vacuum, instead they are largely interdependent with the legitimate economy. Cities with high unemployment rates are populated by people with limited access to the capital need both for extralegal entrepreneurial activities, such as dealing crack, and the capital necessary for purchasing crack as end users. Therefore, such an environment would be a less likely location for the rapid spread of sellers and buyers of crack. In fact, in such a case, high rates of unemployment may act as a buffer against the spread of the homicide epidemic, since the lack of capital retards the diffusion of the profitable illicit behavior linked to lethal violence.

One cautionary note is that when I applied the spline regression techniques to cities without interpolating values for missing data points, the resulting values for the percent change in magnitude differed for some of the cities with missing values (compared to the values without interpolation). This difference was significant enough to alter the best-fitting model reported by AIC. The best-fitting model for the percent change in magnitude in this case was actually the same as the absolute change in magnitude: the best-fitting model only contained the number of cocaine hubs within 500 miles. Since I have elected to include interpolated values for cities with missing data, the analysis is based on the trend lines with these values included.

Table 5.18. Regression Coefficients for the Effects of the Independent Variables on the Latent Duration Variable: Unrestricted Model (Model A) and Best-fitting Model (Model B)

Variables	Model A	Model B
Intercept	69.95	76.78**
(Standard Error)	(48.95)	(16.32)
Density (logged)	-4.65	-7.16**
(Standard Error)	(2.78)	(1.93)
Population (Logged)	-0.96	--
(Standard Error)	(2.97)	--
Resource Deprivation	-3.33	--
(Standard Error)	(11.13)	--
Unemployment	-0.52	--
(Standard Error)	(0.93)	--
Percent Young	0.42	--
(Standard Error)	(0.67)	--
Proximity to Hub	0.01	--
(Standard Error)	(0.01)	--
Number of Hubs within 500 Miles	-0.78	--
(Standard Error)	(0.80)	--
Averaged Homicide Rate	-0.04	--
(Standard Error)	(0.84)	--
Per Capita Police	-<0.01	--
(Standard Error)	(<0.01)	--
N	68	68

-- Variable omitted
* $p < .05$
** $p < .01$

Duration

Table 5.18 presents the results of regressions on the latent duration variable. Again, all of the independent variables (aside from the proximity measures and per capita number of police) are values from circa 1990 (except for St. Petersburg). None of the variables in Model A, the unrestricted model, are significant at the .05 level.

The best-fitting model includes only the population density. However, the direction of the relationship is counter to the expected relationship. The negative relationship between population density and the duration of the homicide epidemic indicates that the greater the population density, the shorter the duration of the epidemic. This is the opposite of the expected relationship. However, this finding may be related to the finding that density was the most important variable for the presence of the epidemic.

Recall that for the presence of the homicide epidemic, the best-fitting model includes only population density and this relationship was positive, the opposite of the relationship between population density and the duration of the epidemic. The finding that population density negatively affected the length of the homicide epidemic could be interpreted as the spread of crack cocaine and the surrounding violence "burning out" more quickly in densely populated cities. A symmetrical social process may have taken place that explains the rise and fall of the homicide epidemic. If the spread of crack cocaine proliferated more readily in densely populated areas, then interest in crack may have also died out more readily than less densely populated areas. Densely populated areas may be better conductors of many kinds of changes in social process, including both increases and decreases of violence. This idea is discussed in greater detail in chapter 6, the concluding chapter of this book.

Conclusion

The purpose of this chapter is to present the characteristics of the variables used in the statistical analysis and also the results of the statistical analysis. The review of variable characteristics presented some surprising findings. For example, consider that overall southern states had the highest poverty levels in 1989, most with rates of 15 percent or greater (U.S. Department of Commerce 1993). However, of the 68 major cities in the sample used in this study, the cities with the highest levels of poverty in 1989 are all found in the East, while the cities with the lowest levels of poverty are actually found in the South, especially the Southwest. The review of city-level characteristics in the sample reveals that the distribution of the independent variables at the city level should be carefully considered when conducting research on this level. Furthermore, the review reveals that cities with high and low levels of the independent variable values tend to cluster in different regions. These findings could be linked to the diffusion of social behavior if the independent variables included in this book affect such behavior.

One of the main purposes of this chapter is to test the effects of key city-level variables on the presence, the absolute change in magnitude, the percent change in magnitude and the duration of the homicide epidemic. The development of theory and research on these dependent variables is in a nascent stage. I conducted statistical tests to determine the significance and strength of bivariate relationships and also to uncover the best-fitting model according to hierarchical nested model comparisons and the use of AIC. I took these steps to determine which variables significantly affected each of the dependent variables and to what degree. I presented and discussed several models for each of the dependent variables.

Overall, the statistical analysis yielded little support for the hypotheses that predicted a significant relationship between key variables associated with homicide rates in general and the epidemic measures. Part of the problem may be attributed to the fact that the theorizing and research on this subject are not well developed. However, I did uncover a number of surprising findings concerning which variables were included in the best-fitting models. The hypotheses presented in chapter 3 were developed from Blumstein's (1995) thesis and predictors of homicide in general. The results of the statistical tests call into question the relationship between cocaine availability and the diffusion of violence.

Population density was the sole best predictor for both the presence of the epidemic and the duration of the epidemic, although the relationship direction and strength of relationship is not consistent. In contrast, the best-fitting models for absolute magnitude and the percent change in magnitude contained completely different variables. Each one also had one significant variable that had a relationship that was the opposite of what was expected. Interestingly, the number of cocaine hubs within 500 miles proved the key predictor for the absolute magnitude of the homicide epidemic, although the relationship was the opposite of what was expected. Still, this is a potentially key finding, since this variable has not yet been included in any scholarly assessment of the homicide epidemic to my knowledge.

This chapter has presented a number of interesting findings concerning characteristics of the homicide epidemic. Some brief explanations for the findings were presented, but I expand my discussion of these findings in the next chapter. I also incorporate these findings into a broader theoretical framework and discuss future lines of research suggested by these new revelations.

CHAPTER 6

The Homicide Epidemic: What We Have Learned and the Next Stage of Inquiry

The goal of this book is to examine three key parameters of the homicide epidemic of the late 1980s and early 1990s. Specifically, the characteristics of the epidemic at the center of this analysis are the presence, magnitude, and duration of the epidemic in major American cities. The analysis included tests of the effects of variables associated with the epidemic and homicide rates in general on these epidemic characteristics.

This chapter concludes the book by providing a summary and discussion of the findings from chapter 5. I review the results of the hypotheses that were tested, discuss the outcome of the tests, and make note of the key findings for each of the epidemic characteristics. I also assess the theoretical arguments drawn from the application of an epidemiological approach to understanding the increase in homicide rates. Finally, I highlight the theoretical and methodological limitations of this book and make recommendations for future research based on the conclusions of the analysis.

Review of Hypotheses

In this chapter I highlight how the hypotheses I tested stood up to the multivariate tests. Nine hypotheses relate to each of the parameters of the epidemic:

1. City population size is positively associated with the parameters of the homicide epidemic.

2. Population density is positively related to the parameters of the epidemic.

3. Resource deprivation is positively associated with the parameters of the epidemic.

4. The unemployment rate is positively associated with the parameters of the epidemic.

5. The percent young is positively associated with the parameters of the epidemic.

6. The proximity to the nearest cocaine hub is positively related to the parameters of the epidemic.

7. The number of cocaine hubs within 500 miles is positively associated with the parameters of the epidemic.

8. The averaged homicide rate variable (average homicide rate 1979-1981) is positively related to the parameters of the homicide epidemic.

9. The per capita number of police is negatively related to the parameters of the epidemic.

Most of these hypotheses were not supported. This result is not altogether surprising considering the parameters of the epidemic under investigation have not received much attention either from theoretical approaches to the epidemic or from research on the homicide epidemic. More generally, criminology lacks a tradition of longitudinal research and theory that seeks to account for rapid change in crime rates (see e.g., La Free 1999).

In many ways the course of this book is akin to grounded theory. What is known about the parameters of the epidemic can only come to light after systematic and rigorous testing of the possible predictors. The test results indicate that a few key variables significantly affected the parameters of the epidemic. However, most of the independent variables did not. Furthermore the interactions effects suggested by the contingent causation theory were also not significant.

Despite the fact that most of the hypotheses were not supported, the tests included in this book do contribute a good deal toward a better understanding of the variables that influenced the diffusion of the epidemic through cities. The contribution of uncovering which variables did not play a significant role in influencing the parameters should not be overlooked. The null findings for a majority of the hypotheses help inform the debate on the variables associated with the epidemic. Below I review the sets of hypotheses for each of the epidemic characteristics individually for each parameter, since the best-fitting model for each varied. I highlight the significant effects and also provide an account of important null effects.

The Presence of the Epidemic

The first parameter of the epidemic included in the statistical analysis is the presence of the epidemic. The overarching question related to this characteristic is: why did some cities experience the epidemic, while others did not? A more refined version of the question is: can social variables explain why some cities experienced the epidemic, while others did not?

The best-fitting model to explain the presence of the epidemic included only population density. The positive relationship between population density and the presence of the epidemic was the lone hypothesis in the set of hypotheses that was supported. This variable was also found significant in prior research on locating the vanguard in rising and falling homicide rates during the epidemic (Messner et al. 2005).

Why is density such an important predictor of the presence of the epidemic? If one uses the analogy of an epidemic of disease a more densely populated city would be more susceptible to an epidemic outbreak than a city with greater distance between potential carriers. The stretch of this analogy to social processes such as those related to new drug acquisition and violent social processes is logical. Consider the adoption of a new product, an introduction into a densely populated city would potentially expose more people, more quickly, than a less densely populated city, even holding the population size constant. This process could be extended to both new recreational drug forms, such as crack, and the diffusion of guns associated with the homicide epidemic. In fact, population density is likely to be a good conductor of any social process that is conveyed from one individual to another.

How can the null effects for the variables aside from population density be accounted for? Although a majority of the hypotheses include variables associated with homicide rates, these variables are mainly found significant in cross-sectional research. While these variables may provide insight into why some areas have higher homicide rates in general, they apparently do not have the same predictive power for determining which cities are more likely to experience a homicide epidemic.

One of the more interesting null effects is the role of population size. Large cities continue to be of central interest for research on the homicide epidemic. However, the statistical results discussed above, which indicate no significant relationship between population size and the parameters of the epidemic suggest that, in fact, students of the homicide epidemic should be more concerned with population density rather than the overall population size. Most likely, vague notions of the importance of "large" cities have masked the importance of population density. What is lacking is reference to why these large cities provide a fertile context for the spread of the homicide epidemic. This distinction is a key contribution of this book since it helps to disentangle what about the populations of large cities makes them more susceptible to epidemics.

The Magnitude of the Epidemic

The second parameter of the homicide epidemic tested was the magnitude of the epidemic. I used two different measures of magnitude in the statistical analysis. The first is absolute magnitude or the absolute difference in homicide rate from the beginning of the epidemic until the end. The second is the percent change in difference from the beginning of the epidemic until the end.

The best-fitting statistical model for predicting the absolute magnitude of the epidemic contains only the number of cocaine hubs within 500 miles. However, the direction of the relationship is the opposite of the expected direction. The number of hubs within 500 miles is *negatively* related to the absolute magnitude. This result means that the higher the density of cocaine hubs within 500 miles the lower the absolute magnitude of the epidemic. Since this finding is in direct contrast to the expected direction stated in the hypothesis, the outcome requires a rethinking of the way cocaine hubs affect the crack market.

Can this contradiction be explained? The original hypothesis was based on the idea that higher cocaine accessibility would translate into more robust crack markets. However, high cocaine accessibility could have a negative effect on the development of crack markets. If participating in black market activities is a rational economic choice, then one would expect more participants when higher profits and lower risks are present. Dealing crack is highly risky behavior. In addition to the dangers of arrest, the death rate among crack dealers is extremely high (Levitt and Venkatesh 2000).

Putting aside any variation in risk, the potential rewards from dealing crack varies widely. The NDIC reports that the cost of a gram of cocaine varies widely depending on geographic location (2000). In areas in which cocaine is relatively less expensive, dealers have less incentive to participate in the high-risk behavior of selling crack. However, this incentive increases as cocaine becomes increasingly expensive, since higher profits may be reaped from the sale of cocaine. Furthermore, in markets that are far from cocaine hubs, to gain a monopolistic hold on the market may be easier, further increasing the profit margin. On the other hand, urban areas served by multiple hubs would be a more difficult marketplace to create and maintain a monopoly. Although the relative costs of cocaine at the city level has not been linked to the growth of the crack market (which is in turn tied to the homicide epidemic) in the literature, the findings concerning the number of hubs within 500 miles and the absolute magnitude of the epidemic should promote a more thorough analysis of the role of the price of cocaine on the crack market.

The second magnitude measure, the percent change in magnitude, yields a different best-fitting model. In this case, two conventional homicide correlates were significantly related: resource deprivation and the unemployment rate. However, the direction of the relationship for each of these variables is different. Resource deprivation met the expectations of the hypothesis and demonstrated positive effects on the percent change in magnitude. On the other hand, the unemployment rate had a negative effect.

How do resource deprivation and the unemployment rate fit into the theoretical framework for the homicide epidemic? First, consider resource deprivation. Access to legitimate means of achieving economic goals is restricted in resource-deprived communities. This restriction can lead to the innovative adaptation of alternative means, including illicit behavior such as selling drugs. The crack epidemic that caused the homicide epidemic would therefore be more likely to spread through a community with high levels of resource deprivation. Furthermore, a resource-deprived community might also be marked by the diffusion of firearms for other reasons besides the introduction of crack.

Even those not involved in illicit activities have restricted access to the police and courts in resource deprived communities. Specifically, one of these restrictions is a level of bias against relying on outsiders (i.e., the police) to resolve interpersonal disputes. Anderson (1999), for example, indicates that the norms of oppositional cultures in inner-city neighborhoods prohibit requesting police intervention and instead encourage violence in some situations to retain respect and avoid future victimization. Sampson and Bartusch (1999) also find support for the idea that residents of resource-deprived neighborhoods tend to champion violence to a greater degree than residents of other neighborhoods.

While the positive effect of resource deprivation meets expectations, the findings for the unemployment rate did not. The multiple regression results reveal that the unemployment rate is negatively associated with the percent change in magnitude. This is consistent with general findings on homicide research. Generally, research indicates inconsistent effects for the unemployment rate on homicide rates (Land et al. 1990). Although the studies reviewed by Land et al. reveal unemployment usually does not have a significant effect on homicide rates, studies that report significance find negative values. In the case of the percent change in magnitude of expected homicide rates, the predicted relationship is positive, following the idea that the unemployed population would be more likely to participate in the crack market. However, the negative results may instead be indicative of lower rates of homicide offense and victimization by the unemployed population based on a routine activities model. If unemployed people spend more time at home, then they are less likely to become involved in the violence surrounding the crack market.

Another possibility is tied to the necessity of money to participate in the crack market. If street-level crack dealers in gangs make around minimum wage (Levitt and Venkatesh 2000), then dealing drugs is a poor way to make a living. Ethnographic research indicates that crack dealers supplement their income with other legitimate jobs (see e.g., Bourgois 1995). Furthermore, money earned from drug dealing used to support drug habits may also be supplemented with money earned from legitimate work.

The interrelationship between the illicit and licit marketplaces could be the cause of the negative relationship between unemployment and the percent change in magnitude of the homicide epidemic. Without the supplemental income from legitimate employment the ability to buy crack and guns is restricted. This restriction could dampen the percent change in the magnitude of homicide rates during the epidemic period.

One final caveat concerns the findings for the percent change in magnitude. Using the dependent variables calculated from the dataset with interpolated values for missing data indicates that the best-fitting model for the percent change in magnitude included only resource deprivation and unemployment. However, the best-fitting model only includes the number of cocaine hubs within 500 miles when the model selection criteria are applied to the data series with no values inserted for missing data (simply applying spline regression techniques to homicide rate trend lines with missing data). This change does not occur for the absolute magnitude, which does not change models regardless correcting for missing data (in both cases the best-fitting model only includes only the number of cocaine hubs within 500 miles). For this reason, the findings for the percent change in magnitude can only be considered tentative at best. Ideally, correcting for missing data with the actual homicide rates for cities with missing data would provide a more solid foundation for the findings.

The Duration of the Epidemic

The last parameter included in statistical analysis is the duration of the epidemic, or how many years the epidemic lasted. The hypotheses for this parameter expect the same relationships as those for the presence and magnitude of the epidemic. The best-fitting statistical model for the duration of the epidemic includes only population density. However, the relationship is negative, which is the opposite of expectations. This negative relationship is an interesting finding and is consistent with a study done on identifying cities in the vanguard of the rising and falling rates of homicide during the epidemic. Messner et al. (2005) found that in bivariate regressions, population density was negatively correlated with the year of downturn in homicide rates at the end of the epidemic. This finding indicates that more densely populated cities experienced the decline in homicide rates prior to less densely populated cities.

A product adoption perspective posits that homicide rates in densely populated cities would not only incline relatively quickly, they would also decline relatively quickly. If the social processes that influence the diffusion of product adoption (such as the adoption of crack) are magnified by the compact nature of densely populated cities, then the diffusion of product rejection may also be magnified in densely populated cites. Perhaps crack was both adopted and rejected more quickly in densely populated cities. Possibly, cities with high population density are more susceptible to rapid social change, regardless of the direction of change.

This one is a key finding of this book, since it highlights another case in which the significant variable that affects changes in homicide rates forces a rethinking of how homicide rates operate during an epidemic. The idea that population density is positively related to homicide rates should be amended for the study of changes in rates during the epidemic, since this research indicates that the relationship between homicide and density is more complex.

Research Limitations

The research presented has limitations that should be made explicit. The limitations can be summed up in two categories: those that affect macro level social research in general and those that are more specific to the approach taken for this study.

The general limitations include variables based on data that are in many respects restricted. This limitation is especially true of the social variables. While I used two different points in time to capture the levels of these variables across the epidemic period, a better dataset would allow for annual (or even monthly) data points. As government agencies continue to refine and expand their data collection they encourage a hopeful future.

However, even the variables that currently have annual data available-such as homicide rates and the number of police per capita-are far from ideal. Relying on the annual change in homicide rates places limits on understanding how quickly rates might diffuse within and between cities across time. The per capita number of police fails to reveal if and how police practices alter homicide rates. If the number of police, or instead, policing practices are the key to homicide rate change, this book can offer no strong support for either side of this debate. Although, in fact, the findings of the statistical analysis reveal that the per capita number of police might not have played an important role in terms of any of the epidemic parameters.

In addition to the general data limitations this study has a number of specific research limitations. First, the theory guiding this research is at an early stage of development, which makes creating hypotheses and extending the research implications difficult. The process of this book has been akin to grounded theory and has required the consideration of a relatively wide set of variables. I selected these variables from research on homicide rates in general and also specifically on the homicide epidemic. However, the method of choosing the best statistical model depended to a greater degree upon statistical techniques rather than a clear theoretical framework.

The calculation of the dependent variables should also be viewed with some caution. Spline regression techniques do offer a method of detecting the systematic portion of trend lines that can allow nonlinear forms as well as detection of significant changes in the regression line. However, these techniques are subject to arbitrary decisions such as the level of significance. I adopted Messner et al.'s (2003) approach of relying on a .05 level of significance, a commonly used level for statistical tests. However, a level of .1 for example would alter the form of the spline regression for some city homicide trends and also therefore alter some of the dependent variable values.

Overall Conclusions

The homicide epidemic of the late 1980s and early 1990s continues to receive attention from students of crime. However, while a few studies have begun the task of uncovering the causes and characteristics of the epidemic, a clear understanding of the epidemic remains elusive. This book can be viewed in the context of an evolving examination of the epidemic. The findings of this book take another step toward disentangling the causes of the homicide epidemic. This final section discusses the most important findings of the research presented in this book.

The three parameters of the epidemic that are the focus of this book have received scant consideration in the literature on the epidemic period. This lack of interest is somewhat surprising, since they represent basic characteristics of the epidemic that should be addressed in the earliest stages of analysis. Much of the prior research has focused on which groups were affected to the greatest degree by the epidemic and testing the connection between the emergence of crack cocaine in urban areas and the subsequent increase homicide rates. However, one of the problems with empirical research on the epidemic is that guiding theory on the causes of the epidemic is not well developed. The weak theoretical framework may be related to the fact that theorizing about rapid changes in crime rates, such as those seen during the epidemic period, is unusual in criminology. The development of a good understanding of the homicide epidemic is in its early stages and will undoubtedly proceed with theoretical developments advancing in tandem with empirical research on the subject.

Research Contributions

One of the most important contributions of this book is the indication that **hypotheses based on the research on general homicide rates are not confirmed when applied to the parameters of the epidemic**. This lack of confirmation may be because theories devised to explain why some cities have higher homicide rates-or why some groups of people are more likely to become homicide victims-are not meant to explain the kinds of rapidly shifting homicide rates associated with the epidemic period. Another reason is that the homicide epidemic period was tied to a relatively short-lived temporal event: the rise and fall of crack cocaine markets within urban areas.

This notion can be tied to arguments that criminologists (and sociologists) know considerably more about events from cross-sectional research than trends from longitudinal research. LaFree (1999) points out that our knowledge of longitudinal data is so rudimentary that we lack even the most basic shared vocabulary to describe changes in trends. For example, La Free introduces the terms crime "boom" and "bust" to identify periods of rapid increases and decreases in homicide rates. In a similar vein, I have opted to adopt the term *epidemic*, a term borrowed from public health, to identify the period of rapid increase in homicides during the late 1980s and early 1990s.

Although the current understanding of crime trends is underdeveloped, such research does offer an opportunity to underscore the value of a sociological approach to crime analysis. Traditional criminological theories, psychological theories, and biological theories cannot explain the rapid increase in homicides that marked the epidemic, nor the rapid decline that followed. Larger cultural trends, in this case the diffusion of crack cocaine, must be considered to provide an explanation of the homicide epidemic.

LaFree (1999) argues that social research is hampered by an ahistorical approach. Considering U.S. homicide trends since WWII, LaFree points out that different periods of increase and decrease can be tied to different cultural trends. The homicide epidemic of the late 80s and 90s appears to be a case in which reference to *ad hoc* cultural trends, such as the introduction of crack, can be tied to rapidly changing homicide rates.

Without the crack epidemic in urban areas, homicide rates would not have exhibited an increase. Grounding changes in crime trends to specific historical periods with reference to the corresponding cultural changes appears to provide the best approach to understanding what fuels changes in crime rates over time. The findings of this book support the idea that specific cultural trends like the distribution of crack cocaine can have significant effects on homicide rates.

One of the surprising findings is that **no significant interaction effects were found between the cocaine measures and the social variables included in the best-fitting statistical model for each of the parameters**. The null effects of the variable interactions may be because the theoretical framework guiding this study fails to identify which variables are most likely to interact with cocaine presence to affect the different parameters. Of course, the theory of contingent causation was not developed to explain variation in the parameters of the epidemic on the city level. Rather, the overarching goal of the theory is to explain why the U.S. has a much greater level of violence associated with drugs than do other Western nations. The null findings for the interaction effects may be another problem tied to the issue of cross-sectional versus longitudinal understanding of crime rates discussed above since the theory of contingent causation may do a good job explaining differences in international levels of violence overall, but not changes in trends.

Another key contribution is the discovery that the predictors of the epidemic parameters are more complex than previously imagined. **While both the presence of the epidemic and the duration of the epidemic were most strongly influenced by population density, the magnitude measures were not**. Furthermore, **the effect of**

population density changed signs, from a positive effect on the presence, to a negative effect on the duration. Additionally, while the finding that the preferred statistical model differed depending on how the magnitude measure was calculated is notable, even more surprising is learning that the number of cocaine hubs within 500 miles was the sole best predictor for the absolute change in magnitude.

This variable has not been included in any other research on the homicide epidemic. However, the findings indicate it is of primary importance to a key parameter of the epidemic. What is also interesting about this particular statistical model is that **the number of cocaine hubs is negatively associated with the absolute magnitude epidemic.** Although this finding runs contrary to expectations, the finding is significant. If the violence surrounding the crack market is sparked by competition over territory and market control, then maybe greater access to cocaine actually serves to ameliorate the violence because incentives to compete fade if the primary resource is more easily obtained and therefore less expensive. Levitt and Venkatesh's (2000) report that street-level gang members make around minimum wage selling crack in Chicago, but wages may be even lower in cities with greater access to cocaine. These lower wages provide a disincentive to run the risks of arrest and violence associated with dealing crack.

More generally, this book can be viewed as providing an important extension to Cork's (1999) city-level test of Blumstein's (1995) theory. Cork found an innovation diffusion pattern that involved both the spread of crack and juvenile firearm homicide. However, this book examines key parameters of the epidemic that are not addressed in Cork's analysis: the presence, magnitude, and duration of the epidemic period. The results uncovered for the parameters underscore the value of research based on the disaggregation of homicide rates to understand what is behind the general pattern, a strategy suggested by McDowall (2002).

Finally, I make one last observation about policing. Interestingly, **the per capita number of police was not a significant predictor in any of the preferred statistical models.** This absence is especially surprising given the consistent reliance on policing to reduce crime. Additionally, policing has repeatedly been cited by politicians, policing agencies, and even some social scientists as a major force behind crime reduction, including the homicide epidemic (see e.g., Kelling and Bratton 1998).

Does policing reduce crime rates?   On one side police administrators and politicians claim their tactics are paying off (although they are conspicuously helpless when crime rates increase). On the other side a long series of research articles report either no effect at all or a slight negative correlation for both the number of police and policing strategies (for a review of the effect of policing on crime see Cameron 1988).

However, contemporary research continues to ponder the role of the police with ever increasing econometric precision. For example, Levitt (1997) employs election cycles as an instrument to measure the effect of policing on crime to overcome the problem of reverse causation. Levitt finds that the number of police does indeed reduce crime.   Furthermore, a recent academic review of policing effectiveness, which favors policing strategies over increasing the number of police, concludes that policing can be effective if is tailored to specific problems (Skogan and Frydl 2004).

Despite expressing support for policing strategy, this same review remarks that the research on policing is limited and often ambiguous. So does policing reduce crime? The answer is that the jury is still out, especially considering the role of policing during the homicide epidemic.

Recently Levitt (2004) authored what appears to be a sort of final word on the causes of the homicide epidemic. He dismisses six factors, including innovative policing strategies, and proclaims four factors to be the best predictors, including increases in the number of police. In his dismissal of policing strategies, he is not alone. A number of studies have highlighted innovative policing tactics and dismissed their role in the declining homicide rates (e.g., Joanes 2000, MacDonald 2002, Rosenfeld et al. 2005). However, the idea that the number of police reduced homicide rates (e.g., Marvell and Moody 1996) has limited support, compelling reasons cast doubt on this relationship. One reason is that Canada, a nation in many respects similar to the United States, experienced crime trends very similar to those of the United States, although in Canada these trends took place without increases in police, incarceration, or innovative police strategies (Ouimet 2002).

As for the evidence found in this book, the number of police is not an important predictor of the homicide epidemic parameters. Perhaps homicide rates and the per capita number of police are simply unrelated. However, another possibility is that policing focused on drugs has contradicting effects on violence. While arresting and incarcerating individual drug dealers may remove individual violent actors from the urban environment, those changes may also serve to exacerbate violence through a number of changes:

1. Policing destabilizes the control of drug markets, resulting in increased violent competition.

2. Policing increases the cost of cocaine, making crack dealing more profitable and, therefore, more attractive than the drug would be without rigorous enforcement.

3. Policing destabilizes social networks by removing young adults from neighborhoods, leaving children without parents, and increasing the economic burden on remaining family members.

While these possibilities demand more thorough research before they are incorporated into a theoretical framework, the potential negative effects of policing should be considered in models that attempt to trace the development of violence surrounding drug markets.

Theoretical Contributions

One of the most important theoretical contributions of this book is the adoption of the epidemiological approach to understanding the rapid homicide rate increases of the late 1980s and early 1990s. The results of the statistical analysis clearly indicate that the homicide predictors identified in cross-sectional homicide research lack predictive power for the parameters of the homicide epidemic. On the other hand, the field of epidemiology has a well-developed set of concepts and a systematic approach to understand rapid increases in disease, which can be extended to the study of homicide trends.

Epidemiology provides a number of important dimensions that can be applied to homicide rate change. Recall from chapter 1 that a common epidemiological definition of an *epidemic* is an "unusually high incidence of a disease where 'unusually high' is fixed in time, in space, and in the persons afflicted as compared with previous experience" (Hagget 2000: 2). One key dimension that should be incorporated into the study of homicide is time. Just as an increase in disease cannot be understood without reference to the relative levels of disease before the onset of the increase, an increase in homicide rates cannot be understood without understanding the relative trend in rates. I have overcome this problem in this study by considering longitudinal homicide rate trends.

Other dimensions identified in the definition can also be applied to homicide research. Consider spatial relationships. We know that urban areas were affected to a greater degree than suburban areas (see e.g., Grogger and Willis 2000). The homicide epidemic appears to have diffused from coastal areas toward the Midwest (Cork 1999, Messner et al. 2005). The idea that homicide rate increases can spread geographically has received some limited attention, but is an important consideration in terms of the interrelationships between spatially related populations.

Thinking about homicide from an epidemiological perspective also introduces the idea of contagions and susceptibility. Is the diffusion of homicide tied to the spread of identifiable antecedents? The homicide epidemic of the late 1980s and early 1990s, for example, is tied to the spread of crack and the distribution of handguns. Identifying the potential predictors of homicide rate increases can help reveal why homicide rates are changing and which public policy efforts might reduce the impact of inclining rates.

Finally, an epidemiological perspective helps us to accept the idea that homicide rates can change direction and rate of change quickly. Traditional linear regression cannot capture quadratic and cubic changes that can accompany rapid rate changes. Non-linear rate structures must be considered, especially for smaller geographical units such as cities.

Although the development of theory to explain the homicide epidemic is still in the early stages, the results of this book suggest a number of changes to the way the homicide epidemic is thought about including:

1. Moving beyond vague notions of the role of a few "large" cities. Clearly, the epidemic affected cities across the country and was not restricted to only the largest.

2.   Recognizing the importance of density. While population density and size often "hang together" in community level research on homicide rates (Land et al. 1990), this link may not be the case for the parameters of the homicide epidemic. Understanding how population density affected the diffusion of violence deserves attention and should be the focus of future research.

3.   Considering the national diffusion of cocaine. Although studies have found support for Blumstein's (1995) thesis that the crack epidemic lead to the homicide epidemic, a clear understanding of the role of cocaine diffusion has not been incorporated into the theory. The number of cocaine hubs within 500 miles is the fundamental predictor for the absolute change in the magnitude of homicide rates during the epidemic. Although law enforcement agencies recognize that cocaine availability and cost vary widely across the country, the effects of this variation on the parameters of the homicide epidemic not been fully considered.

4.   Recognizing that conventional community-level homicide research offers limited explanatory power for the epidemic. Predictors of homicide rates in general did not perform well under statistical scrutiny. The homicide epidemic requires explanations that move beyond traditional homicide rate predictors. The analysis of the epidemic needs to approach an unusual event with unconventional explanations.

Future Research

I have several recommendations for future research based upon the findings of this book. These recommendations include both general and specific recommendations. First, I will discuss the general recommendations, and then I will go on to highlight several specific extensions of this book.

This book, although heavily influenced by the sociological perspective, is reflective of criminology in general, borrowing from various academic fields including public health and economics. This multidisciplinary approach has resulted in a more rigorous analysis than simply adopting a singular approach taken from one field of study. The epidemiological approach provides concepts and a way of thinking about rapidly changing rates that is systematic and grounded in a tradition of research on how public health problems diffuse through geographical areas. On the other hand, this book has been limited by the fact that the data analysis is completely based on city-level variables derived from official data. This poses some major limitations on what can be learned about the homicide epidemic parameters.

While this research on the city-level does provide a better idea of the variables that influenced the epidemic parameters, a good understanding of the actual social processes that took place is still lacking. For example, why is density the primary predictor for both the parameters and the duration of the epidemic? Maybe the social process of accepting new innovations, such as crack, diffuses more quickly through densely populated areas. Furthermore, the rejection of crack may also have diffused more quickly through densely populated areas. But the processes by which crack diffused through cities are not readily apparent. Very few studies look at the patterns of diffusion tied to the process of drug adoption in urban areas (or comparative research on non-urban areas) although such research may reveal a great deal about changes in rates of drug use and violence.

One of the most interesting findings uncovered by this research is the role of multiple access channels for cocaine. A city with many cocaine hubs within 500 miles is more likely to experience a smaller absolute change in homicide rates. Exactly why this is true is unclear. Perhaps the effect of cocaine availability is linked to the rational choices made by individuals who must weigh the risk of arrest and violence versus the potential profit from selling crack, a choice influenced by the availability and cost of cocaine. Again, criminologists have not looked closely at the effects of the roles of drug availability and pricing on the diffusion of drug markets and violence within cities and across geographical areas.

The dominant theory to explain the homicide epidemic includes the diffusion of crack and the diffusion of firearms. However, the declining rates in homicide following the epidemic took place in an environment that was already saturated with guns. What process lead to a de-escalation of the arms race? Perhaps the de-escalation linked to a de-escalation in the violence surrounding the crack market, although how and why this occurred is not yet understood. The processes that lead to a cultural shift away from violence demand better explanations.

Finally, an important general theme emerges from the findings of this book: the importance of time and space in understanding how homicide rates operate. This theme brings to light a number of points. The affect of variables on homicide rates may vary during specific historical periods (e.g., the spread of crack cocaine and the homicide epidemic). Cross sectional research cannot account for such variation. In a related vein, the notion that rate changes may diffuse across geographical areas in a patterned fashion is also key to understanding the operation of the homicide epidemic and should be considered for other historical periods and types of violence. Additionally, the extent to which the interconnections of geographical areas affect rate changes is still not well understood. This book focuses specifically on the United States, but I have no good reason to suspect that such diffusion ends at national boundaries. Even within the United States, no research has revealed if cities other than the largest American cities also played a role in the homicide diffusion.

Here is a list of specific research recommendations drawn from this study:

1. Expand the test of homicide parameters to include cities other than the largest American cities. We do not know how mid-sized and smaller cities experienced the homicide epidemic.

2. Expand the test of homicide parameters to look carefully at other historical periods of homicide rate incline. The idea of considering rate increases as epidemics is relatively new and may have implications for other historical periods.

3. Consider international homicide rate trends. Starting with Canadian and Mexican data, we should determine if and how homicide rates might have diffused across national boundaries. Such research could also be extended internationally to other countries that may have experienced similar crime trend changes.

4. Incorporate and improve measures of availability and cost of cocaine in relation to the homicide rate parameters. Although data on these variables are limited, the findings of this book support the incorporation of such measures.

5. Refine and include measures of policing policy to determine the effect on homicide rate trends. Using measures of police

practice by looking at the number of arrests for drug crimes per police officer, for example, might help clarify the role of policing strategies and homicide rate parameters.

This book has revealed some surprising findings. Incorporating the findings and extending the scope of research across space and time will help us come to a better understanding of how homicide rates operate and such research may also help inform us about what actions may retard the spread of future homicide epidemics.

APPENDICES

Appendix A. Dependent Variables in Models Included in Goodness-of-Fit Tests

A

Population Density (Logged)
Population (Logged)
Resource Deprivation Index
Unemployment Rate
Percent Young
Proximity to Nearest Cocaine Hub
Number of Hubs within 500 Miles
Averaged Homicide Rate 1979-81
Police Per Capita

B

Population Density (Logged)
Population (Logged)
Resource Deprivation Index
Unemployment Rate
Percent Young
Proximity to Nearest Cocaine Hub
Number of Hubs within 500 Miles
Averaged Homicide Rate 1979-81

C

Population Density (Logged)
Population (Logged)
Resource Deprivation Index
Unemployment Rate
Percent Young
Proximity to Nearest Cocaine Hub
Number of Hubs within 500 Miles

Appendix A. Dependent Variables in Models Included in Goodness-of-Fit Tests (Continued)

D
Population Density (Logged)
Population (Logged)
Resource Deprivation Index
Unemployment Rate
Percent Young
Proximity to Nearest Cocaine Hub

E
Population Density (Logged)
Population (Logged)
Resource Deprivation Index
Unemployment Rate
Percent Young

F
Population Density (Logged)
Population (Logged)
Resource Deprivation Index
Unemployment Rate

G
Population Density (Logged)
Population (Logged)
Resource Deprivation Index

H
Population Density (Logged)
Population (Logged)

Appendix A. Dependent Variables in Models Included in Goodness-of-Fit Tests (Continued)

I
Population Density (Logged)

J
Population (Logged)
Resource Deprivation Index
Unemployment Rate
Percent Young

Proximity to Nearest Cocaine Hub
Number of Hubs within 500 Miles
Averaged Homicide Rate 1979-81
Police Per Capita

K
Population (Logged)
Resource Deprivation Index
Unemployment Rate
Percent Young
Proximity to Nearest Cocaine Hub
Number of Hubs within 500 Miles
Averaged Homicide Rate 1979-81

L
Population (Logged)
Resource Deprivation Index
Unemployment Rate
Percent Young
Proximity to Nearest Cocaine Hub
Number of Hubs within 500 Miles

Appendix A. Dependent Variables in Models Included in Goodness-of-Fit Tests (Continued)

M
Population (Logged)
Resource Deprivation Index
Unemployment Rate
Percent Young
Proximity to Nearest Cocaine Hub

N
Population (Logged)
Resource Deprivation Index
Unemployment Rate
Percent Young

O
Population (Logged)
Resource Deprivation Index
Unemployment Rate

P
Population (Logged)
Resource Deprivation Index

Q
Population (Logged)

Appendix A. Dependent Variables in Models Included in Goodness-of-Fit Tests (Continued)

R

Resource Deprivation Index
Unemployment Rate
Percent Young
Proximity to Nearest Cocaine Hub
Number of Hubs within 500 Miles
Averaged Homicide Rate 1979-81
Police Per Capita

S

Resource Deprivation Index
Unemployment Rate
Percent Young
Proximity to Nearest Cocaine Hub
Number of Hubs within 500 Miles
Averaged Homicide Rate 1979-81

T

Resource Deprivation Index
Unemployment Rate
Percent Young
Proximity to Nearest Cocaine Hub
Number of Hubs within 500 Miles

U

Resource Deprivation Index
Unemployment Rate
Percent Young
Proximity to Nearest Cocaine Hub

Appendix A. Dependent Variables in Models Included in Goodness-of-Fit Tests (Continued)

V
Resource Deprivation Index
Unemployment Rate
Percent Young

W
Resource Deprivation Index
Unemployment Rate

X
Resource Deprivation Index

Y
Unemployment Rate
Percent Young
Proximity to Nearest Cocaine Hub
Number of Hubs within 500 Miles
Averaged Homicide Rate 1979-81
Police Per Capita

Z
Unemployment Rate
Percent Young
Proximity to Nearest Cocaine Hub
Number of Hubs within 500 Miles
Averaged Homicide Rate 1979-81

Appendix A. Dependent Variables in Models Included in Goodness-of-Fit Tests (Continued)

AA
Unemployment Rate
Percent Young

Proximity to Nearest Cocaine Hub
Number of Hubs within 500 Miles

AB
Unemployment Rate
Percent Young
Proximity to Nearest Cocaine Hub

AC
Unemployment Rate
Percent Young

AD
Unemployment Rate

AE
Percent Young
Proximity to Nearest Cocaine Hub
Number of Hubs within 500 Miles
Averaged Homicide Rate 1979-81
Police Per Capita

AF
Percent Young
Proximity to Nearest Cocaine Hub
Number of Hubs within 500 Miles
Averaged Homicide Rate 1979-81

Appendix A. Dependent Variables in Models Included in Goodness-of-Fit Tests (Continued)

AG
Percent Young
Proximity to Nearest Cocaine Hub

Number of Hubs within 500 Miles

AH
Percent Young
Proximity to Nearest Cocaine Hub

AI
Percent Young

AJ
Proximity to Nearest Cocaine Hub
Number of Hubs within 500 Miles
Averaged Homicide Rate 1979-81
Police Per Capita

AK
Proximity to Nearest Cocaine Hub
Number of Hubs within 500 Miles
Averaged Homicide Rate 1979-81
AL
Proximity to Nearest Cocaine Hub
Number of Hubs within 500 Miles

AM
Proximity to Nearest Cocaine Hub

Appendix A. Dependent Variables in Models Included in Goodness-of-Fit Tests (Continued)

AN
Number of Hubs within 500 Miles
Averaged Homicide Rate 1979-81
Police Per Capita

AO
Number of Hubs within 500 Miles
Averaged Homicide Rate 1979-81

AP
Number of Hubs within 500 Miles

AQ
Averaged Homicide Rate 1979-81
Police Per Capita

AR
Averaged Homicide Rate 1979-81

AS
Police Per Capita

Appendix B. Models with AIC Values for the Presence of the Epidemic

Model	AIC Score
A	96.57
B	95.73
C	94.58
D	96.93
E	95.24
F	93.31
G	91.52
H	90.07
I	88.88* *Best-fitting Model
J	93.83
K	96.60
L	95.39
M	98.28
N	96.28
O	95.62
P	93.68
Q	94.05
R	92.68
S	95.94
T	95.22
U	97.86
V	96.01
W	95.54
X	93.59
Y	94.15
Z	94.40
AA	97.15
AB	99.10
AC	97.22
AD	96.34

Appendix B. Models with AIC Values for the Presence of the Epidemic (continued)

Model	AIC Score
AE	92.30
AF	92.87
AG	95.24
AH	98.72
AI	97.41
AJ	91.10
AK	91.83
AL	93.75
AM	97.43
AN	90.35
AO	90.28
AP	91.91
AQ	92.80
AR	94.06
AS	90.88

Appendix C. Models with AIC Values for the Absolute Magnitude of the Epidemic

Model	AIC Score
A	331.63
B	329.64
C	328.64
D	330.06
E	328.12
F	326.21
G	329.44
H	330.18
I	328.18
J	332.49
K	328.63
L	327.72
M	330.26
N	328.34
O	326.72
P	332.10
Q	331.52
R	330.51
S	327.10
T	325.98
U	328.53
V	326.71
W	324.71
X	331.17
Y	328.89
Z	326.55
AA	328.63
AB	332.19
AC	330.68
AD	329.01

Appendix C. Models with AIC Values for the Absolute Magnitude of the Epidemic

Model	AIC Score
AE	330.43
AF	327.80
AG	327.32
AH	332.28
AI	332.21
AJ	329.00
AK	326.19
AL	325.58
AM	330.31
AN	327.01
AO	324.19
AP	323.59* Best-fitting Model
AQ	332.74
AR	331.36
AS	331.08

Appendix D. Models with AIC Values for % Change in Magnitude of the Epidemic

Model	AIC Score
A	393.15
B	391.18
C	393.42
D	393.65
E	391.65
F	389.71
G	396.57
H	395.67
I	396.16
J	391.88
K	390.18
L	392.66
M	392.52
N	390.64
O	389.75
P	395.22
Q	394.45
R	391.18
S	389.64
T	392.88
U	392.64
V	390.64
W	389.17* Best-fitting Model
X	395.38
Y	395.91
Z	395.79
AA	394.03
AB	394.86
AC	392.93
AD	391.45

Appendix D. Models with AIC Values for % Change in Magnitude of the Epidemic

Model	AIC Score
AE	394.87
AF	394.47
AG	393.35
AH	395.00
AI	393.79
AJ	397.18
AK	395.90
AL	394.93
AM	395.41
AN	395.19
AO	393.93
AP	392.94
AQ	395.63
AR	395.34
AS	395.16

Appendix E. Models with AIC Values for the Duration of the Epidemic

Model	AIC Score
A	318.69
B	316.70
C	315.08
D	314.96
E	313.65
F	312.04
G	310.41
H	309.56
I	308.29* Best-fitting Model
J	318.24
K	317.58
L	315.87
M	317.05
N	315.08
O	316.67
P	316.39
Q	317.35
R	316.32
S	317.92
T	316.55
U	317.57
V	315.63
W	318.26
X	318.48
Y	317.48
Z	316.06
AA	315.73
AB	316.28
AC	314.29
AD	317.14

Appendix E. Models with AIC Values for the Duration of the Epidemic

Model	AIC Score
AE	316.91
AF	315.57
AG	318.94
AH	321.68
AI	321.37
AJ	315.80
AK	314.80
AL	317.71
AM	320.80
AN	314.09
AO	312.86
AP	315.71
AQ	317.34
AR	317.55
AS	317.17

REFERENCES

Anderson, Elijah. 1990. *Streetwise*. Chicago: University of Chicago Press.

Bailey, William C. 1984. "Poverty, Inequality, and City Homicide Rates." *Criminology* 22:531-550.

Baumer, Eric P. 1994. "Poverty, Crack, and Crime: A Cross-City Analysis." *Journal of Research in Crime and Delinquency* 31: 311-327.

Baumer, Eric P., Janet L. Lauritsen, Richard Rosenfeld, and Richard Wright. 1998. "The Influence of Crack Cocaine on Robbery, Burglary, and Homicide Rates: A Cross-City, Longitudinal Analysis." *Journal of Research in Crime and Delinquency* 35: 316-340.

Belenko, Steven R. 1993. *Crack and the Evolution of Anti-Drug Policy*. Westport, Connecticut: Greenwood Press.

Belsley, David A., Edwin Kuh, and Roy E. Welsh. 1980. *Regression diagnostics: Identifying influential data and sources of collinearity*. New York: John Wiley and Sons.

Bennett, William, John Dilulio, and John Walters. 1996. *Body Count*. New York: Simon and Schuster.

Benenson, Abraham S. (ed.). 1990. *Control of Communicable Diseases in Man (15th edition)*. Washington, D.C.: American Public Health Association.

Blumstein, Alfred. 1995. "Youth Violence, Guns, and the Illicit-Drug Industry." *Journal of Criminal Law and Criminology* 86:10-36.

Blumstein, Alfred. 2000. "Disaggregation Violence Trends." Pp. 13-44 in *The Crime Drop in America*, edited by Alfred Blumstein and Joel Wallman.

Blumstein, Alfred, Jacqueline Cohen, and Harold Miller. "Demographically Disaggregated Projections of the Prison Population." *Journal of Criminal Justice* 8:1-25.

Blumstein, Alfred and Richard Rosenfeld 1998. "Explaining Recent Trends in U.S. Homicide Rates." *Journal of Criminal Law and Criminology* 88:1175-1216.

Blumstein, Alfred and Joel Wallman. 2000. "The Recent Rise and Fall of American Violence." Pp. 1-12 in *The Crime Drop in America*, edited by Alfred Blumstein and Joel Wallman.

Bourgois, Philip 1995. *In Search of Respect: Selling Crack in El Barrio*. Cambridge: Cambridge University Press.

Cameron, Samuel. 1988. "The Economics of Crime Deterrence: A Survey of Theory and Evidence." *Kyklos* 41: 301-323.

Cone, Edward J. 1995. "Pharmacokinetics and Pharmacodynamics of Cocaine." *Journal of Analytical Toxicology* 19:459-478.

Conklin, John E. 2003. *Why Crime Rates Fell*. Boston: Allyn and Bacon.

Cook, Phillip J. and John H. Laub. 1998. "After the Epidemic: Recent Trends in Youth Violence in the United States." Pp. 1-37 in *Crime and Justice: A Review of Research*, Vol. 29, edited by Michael Tonry. Chicago: University of Chicago Press.

Cooper, Mary H. 1990. *The Business of Drugs*. Washington, D.C.: Congressional Quarterly Inc.

Cork, Daniel. 1999. "Examining Space-Time Interaction in City-Level Homicide Data: Crack Markets and the Diffusion of Guns Among Youth." *Journal of Quantitative Criminology* 15:379-406.

Demaris, Alfred. 1995. "A Tutorial in Logisitic Regression." *Journal of Marriage and Family* 67:956-969.

Donohue, John and Steven Levitt. 2001. "Legalized Abortion and Crime." *Quarterly Journal of Economics* 116 (2): 379-420.

Durkheim, Émile. 1951 [1897]. *Suicide*. London: Routledge.

Easterlin, Richard A. 1978. "What Will 1984 Be Like? Socioeconomic Implications of Recent Twists in Age Structure." *Demography* 15:397-421.

Easterlin, Richard A. 1987. *Birth and Fortune: The impact of Numbers on Personal Welfare, 2nd Edition.* Chicago: University of Chicago Press.

Eck, John E. and Edward R. Maguire. 2000. "Have Changes in Policing Reduced Violent Crime? An Assessment of the Evidence." Pp. 207-265 in *The Crime Drop in America*, edited by Alfred Blumstein and Joel Wallman. Cambridge: Cambridge University Press.

Fishman, Mark. 1978. "Crime Waves as Ideology." *Social Problems* 25:531-43.

Fox, James A. 1978. *Forecasting Crime Data: An Econometric Analysis*. Lexington, MA: Lexington Books.

Fox, James A.. 2000. "Demographics in U.S. Homicide." Pp. 288-317 in *The Crime Drop in America*, edited by Alfred Blumstein and Joel Wallman. Cambridge: Cambridge University Press.

Fox, James Alan and Jack Levin. 2000. *The Will to Kill: Making Sense of Senseless Murder*. Needham Heights, MA: Allyn and Bacon.

Fryer, Roland G., Paul S. Heaton, Steven D. Levitt, and Kevin M. Murphy. *Measuring the Impact of Crack Cocaine*. National Bureau of Economic Research, Inc: Working Paper 11318.

Goldstein, Paul J. 1985. "The Drugs/Violence Nexus: A Tripartite Conceptual Framework." *Journal of Drug Issues* 14:493-506.

Goode, Erich and Nachman Ben-Yehuda. 1994. *Moral Panics: The Social Construction of Deviance.* Cambridge, Massachusetts: Blackwell Publishers.

Gladwell, Malcolm. 2000. *The Tipping Point: How Little Things Can Make a Big Difference.* Boston, Massachusetts: Little, Brown.

Greenberg, David F. 1985. "Age, Crime, and Social Explanation." *American Journal of Sociology* 91:1-21.

Grogger, Jeff. 2000. "An Economic Model of Recent Trends in Violence." Pp. 266-287 in *The Crime Drop in America*, edited by Alfred Blumstein and Joel Wallman. Cambridge: Cambridge University Press.

Grogger, Jeff and Michael Willis. 2000. "The Emergence of Crack Cocaine and the Rise in Urban Crime Rates." *The Review of Economics and Statistics* 82: 519-529.

Gujerati 1995. *Basic Econometrics, 3rd Edition.* NewYork: McGraw-Hill.

Hagget, Peter. 2000. *The Geographical Structure of Epidemics.* Oxford: Clarendon Press.

Hansen, Bruce E. 2001. "The New Econometrics of Structural Change: Dating Breaks in U.S. Labor Productivity." *Journal of Economic Perspectives* 15:117-128.

Hirshi, Travis and Michael Gottfredson. 1983. "Age and the Explanation of Crime." *The American Journal of Sociology* 89:552-584.

Jaccard, James. 2001. *Interaction Effects in Logistic Regression.* Thousand Oaks, CA: Sage.

Joanes, Ana. 2000. "Does the New York City Police Department Deserve Credit for the Decline in New York City's Homicide Rates? A Cross-City Comparison of Policing Strategies and Homicide Rates." *Columbia Journal of Law and Social Problems* 33:265-311.

Johnson, Bruce D., Andrew Golub and Eloise Dunlap. "The Rise and Decline of Hard Drugs, Drug Markets, and Violence in Inner-City New York." Pp. 164-206 in *The Crime Drop in America*, edited by Alfred Blumstein and Joel Wallman. Cambridge: Cambridge University Press.

Jones, Marshall B. and Donald R. Jones. 2000. "The Contagious Nature of Anti-Social Behavior." *Criminology* 38:25-46.

Kelling, George L., Tony Pate, Duane Dieckman, and Charles Brown. 1974. The Kansas City Preventative Patrol Experiment: A Summary Report. Police Foundation: Washington, D.C.

Kelling, George L. and Catherine M. Coles. 1996. Fixing Broken Windows: Restoring Order and Reducing Crime in Our Communities. Touchstone: New York City

Kelling, George L. and William J. Bratton. 1998. "Declining Crime Rates: Insiders' Views of the New York City Story." *Journal of Criminal Law and Criminology* 88:1217-1231.

Krivo, Lauren J. and Ruth D. Peterson. 1996. "Extremely Disadvantaged Neighborhoods and Urban Crime." *Social Forces* 75:619-649.

La Free, Gary. 1999. "Declining Violent Crime Rates in the 1990s: Predicting crime Booms and Busts." *Annual Review of Sociology* 25:145-168.

Land, Kenneth C., Patricia L. McCall, and Lawrence E. Cohen. 1990. "Structural Covariates of Homicide Rates: Are There Any Invariances across Time and Social Space?" *American Journal of Sociology* 95:922-963.

Lee, Matthew R. 2000. Concentrated Poverty, Race, and Homicide. Sociological Quarterly 41:189-206.

Levitt, Steven D. 1997. "Using Electoral Cycles in Police Hiring to Estimate the Effects of Police on Crime." *American Economic Review* 87: 270-290.

Levitt, Steven D. 2002. "Using Electoral Cycles in Police Hiring to Estimate the Effects of Police on Crime: Reply." *American Economic Review* 92: 1244-1250.

Levitt, Steven D. 2004. "Understanding Why Crime Fell in the 1990s: Four Factors That Explain the Decline and Six That Do Not." *Journal of Economic Perspectives* 18:163-190.

Levitt, Steven D. and Sudhir Alladi Venkatesh. 2000 "An Economic Analysis of a Drug-Selling Gang's Finances." *The Quarterly Journal of Economics* 115: 755-789.

Marsh, Lawrence C. 1986. "Estimating the Number and Location of Knots in Spline Regressions." *Journal of Applied Business Research* 3:60-70.

Marsh, Lawrence C., and David R.Cormier. 2001. *Spline Regression Models*. Sage University Papers Series on Quantitative Applications in the Social Sciences, 07-137. Thousand Oaks, CA.: Sage.

McDowall, David. 2002. "Tests of Nonlinear Dynamics in U.S. Homicide Time Series, and Their Implications." *Criminology* 40:711-735.

Messner, Steven F. 1982. "Societal Development, Social Equality, and Homicide: A Cross-National Test of a Durkheimian Model." *Social Forces* 61:225-240.

Messner, Steven F., Glenn Deane, Luc Anslin, and Benjamin Pearson-Nelson. 2003. "Locating the Vanguard in Rising and Falling Homicide Rates." Unpublished Paper Presented at the Fifty-fifth Annual Meeting of the American Society of Criminology.

Mieczkowski, Thomas. 1990. "Crack distribution in Detroit." *Contemporary Drug Problems* 17:9-30.

Moore, Mark H.1995. "Public Health and Criminal Justice Prevention." Pp. 237-262 in *Building a Safer Society: Strategic Approaches to Crime Prevention.* Chicago: The University of Chicago Press.

Moore, Mark H. and Michael Tonry. 1998. "Youth Violence in America". In *Youth Violence.* Edited by Michael Tonry and Mark H. Moore. Chicago: The University of Chicago Press.

Morenoff, Jeffery D. and Robert J. Samson. 1997. "Violent Crime and the Spatial Dynamics of Neighborhood Transition: Chicago, 1970-1990." *Social Forces* 76:31-65.

National Drug Intelligence Center. 2001. National Drug Threat Assessment. Retrieved online at: http://www.usdoj.gov/ndic/pubs/647/cocaine.htm#Foot4

O'Brien, Robert M, Jean Stockard, and Lynne Isaacson. 1999. "The Enduring Effects of Cohort Characteristics on Age-Specific Homicide Rates, 1960-1995." *American Journal of Sociology* 104:1061-1095.

O'Brien, Robert M. and Jean Stockard. 2003. "The Cohort-Size Sample-Size Conundrum: An Empirical Analysis and Assessment Using Homicide Arrest Data from 1960 to 1999." *Journal of Quantitative Criminology* 19:1-32.

Ousey, Graham C. 1999. "Homicide, Structural Factors, and the Racial Invariance Assumption." *Criminology* 37:405-426.

Ousey, Graham and Mathew R. Lee. 2002. "Examining the Conditional Nature of the Illicit Drug Market-Homicide Relationship: A Partial Test of the Theory of Contingent Causation." *Criminology* 40:73-102.

Palen, J. John. 2005. *The Urban World.* McGraw-Hill: New York.

Parker, Karen F. and Patricia L. McCall. 1999. "Structural Conditions and Racial Homicide Patterns: A Look at the Multiple Disadvantages in Urban Areas." *Criminology* 37:447-477.

Rosenfeld, Richard. 2002. "Crime Decline in Context." *Contexts: Understanding People in Their Social Worlds* 1:25-34.

Sampson, Robert J. 1987. "Urban Black Violence: The Effect of Male Joblessness and Family Disruption." *American Journal of Sociology* 93:348-382.

Sampson, Robert J. and Dawn Jeglum Bartusch. 1999. Attitudes Toward Crime, Police, and the Law: Individual and Neighborhood Differences. Washington, D.C.: U.S. Department of Justice, National Institute of Justice.

Sampson, R.J., and Lauritsen, J.L. 1994. "Violent victimization and offending: Individual-, situational-, and community-level risk factors." In *Understanding and Preventing Violence,* vol. 3, edited by A.J. Reiss and J.A. Roth. Washington, DC: National Academy Press, pp. 1–114.

Sampson, Robert J. and Stephen W. Raudenbush. 1997. "Neighborhoods and Violent Crime: A Multilevel Study of Collective Efficacy." *Science* 277:918-25.

Sampson, Robert J. and Jacqueline Cohen. 1988. "Deterrent Effects of the Police on Crime: A Replication and Theoretical Extension." Law and Society Review 22:162-189

Steffensmeier, Darrell, Emilie Allan, Miles Harer, and Cathy Streifel. 1989. "Age and the Distribution of Crime." *American Journal of Sociology* 94:803-831.

Tarde, Gabriel. 1903. *The Laws of Imitation.* New York: Holt.

Tobin, James. 1958. "Estimation of Relationships for Limited Dependent Variables." *Econometrica* 26: 24-36.

Tonry, Michael and Mark H. Moore. 1998. "Youth Violence in

America" in *Youth Violence*, edited by Michael Tonry and Mark H. Moore.

U.S. Bureau of Labor Statistics. 2004. "Explanatory Notes and Estimates of Error" in *Employment and Earnings*, February.

U.S. Department of Justice. 1979-2001. Federal Bureau of Investigation. (Volumes from1979 to 2001). Crime in the United States: Uniform Crime Reports. Washington: USGPO.

U. S. Department of Justice. 2004. Homicide Trends in the U. S. Bureau of Justice Statistics. Retrieved online at http://www.ojp.usdoj.gov/bjs/homicide/hmrt.htm

U. S. Department of Commerce. 1983. *County and City Data Book*. Bureau of the Census.

U. S. Department of Commerce. 1993. *Statistical Brief: Poverty in the United States- Changes between the Censuses*. Bureau of the Census.

U. S. Department of Commerce. 1994. *County and City Data Book*. Bureau of the Census.

Wilson, William Julius. 1987. *The Truly Disadvantaged: The Inner-city, the Underclass, and Public Policy*. Chicago: The University of Chicago Press.

Wilson, William Julius. 1996. *When Work Disappears: The World of the New Urban Poor:* New York: Knopf.

Wilson, James Q. and Barbara Boland. 1978. "The Effect of the Police on Crime." *Law and Society Review* 12:367-90.

Wilson, James Q. and George L. Kelling. 1982. "The Police and Neighborhood Safety." Atlantic Monthly (March):29-38.

Zimring, Franklin and Gordon Hawkins. 1997. *Crime is not the Problem: Lethal Violence in America.* Oxford: Oxford University Press.

INDEX

Johnson, 64, 92
Jones, 62
Kelling, 8, 50, 232
Krivo, 80
Kuh, 176
La Free, 62, 213, 228
Land, 73, 80, 81, 112, 113,
  220, 237
Laub, 3, 6, 7, 9, 10, 20, 30, 75,
  141, 164
Lee, 8, 32, 33, 64, 65, 80, 92,
  113
Levin, 32
Levitt, 8, 17, 50, 119, 180,
  218, 221, 231, 233
logistic regression, 14, 101,
  196
Maguire, 17
Marsh, 97
McCall, 80
McDowall, 62, 63, 232
Messner, 11, 13, 14, 20, 63,
  65, 66, 70, 71, 73, 95, 96,
  98, 99, 102, 111, 113, 115,
  140, 141, 163, 174, 178,
  182, 184, 215, 223, 226, 236
Mieczkowski, 35
Moore, 6, 7, 21, 23, 40, 41
Morenoff, 80
O'Brien, 8, 76
Ousey, 8, 32, 33, 64, 65, 80,
  92, 113
outbreak, 1, 2, 6, 21, 23, 30,
  41, 215
Palen, 73
Parker, 80
Peterson, 80
policing, 8, 12, 17, 50, 51, 53,
  56, 57, 58, 73, 82, 89, 119,
  166, 167, 225, 232, 233,

234, 235
public health, 2, 5, 6, 23, 30,
  40, 228, 239
Rosenfeld, 3, 7, 20, 49, 233
routine activities theory, 22
Sampson, 55, 80, 220
social disorganization theory,
  3, 22
spline regression, 13, 95, 96,
  102, 103, 104, 118, 122,
  123, 126, 127, 129, 130,
  203, 222, 226
Steffensmeier, 75
Stockard, 8
suicide, 23, 24, 27
Tarde, 24, 27, 28, 29
Tobin, 99, 100
Tobit regression, 99, 106, 190
Tonry, 6, 7, 21, 40, 41
Venkatesh, 218, 221, 231
Wallman, 7, 49
Walters, 75
Willis, 8, 34, 64, 65, 66, 67,
  92, 236
Wilson, 50, 80, 180
Zimring, 3, 4, 10, 11, 12, 45,
  46, 47, 48, 53, 58, 80, 88,